A FRESH VISION

A CALL TO THE CHURCH TO RETURN TO THE PREACHING OF BIBLICAL
SALVATION AND A CASE AGAINST CALVINISM

Rev. Rodger C. Moyer

Author of
The Apostles' Creed
The Last Days and Rapture of the Church
What They Had We Need
What We Need to Know and Never Let Go

SCHMUL PUBLISHING COMPANY
NICHOLASVILLE, KENTUCKY

Cover image copyright: <a href="https://www.123rf.com/profile_stillfx">stillfx / 123RF Stock Photo</a>. Used by permission.

Published by Schmul Publishing Co.
PO Box 776
Nicholasville, KY 40340
USA

Printed in the United States of America

ISBN 10: 0-88019-629-7
ISBN 13: 978-0-88019-629-1

Visit us on the Internet at www.wesleyanbooks.com, or order direct from the publisher by calling 800-772-6657, or by writing to the above address.

Contents

Preface

IT'S BEEN A LITTLE while since I've written a book and things have changed much in my life since the last one. In 2016 I began preparing messages for my church entitled "A Fresh Vision." I was concerned with the seeming loss of the sense of sin, and the power of God's plan of salvation to deliver people from their sins and the sin nature itself. It had seemed to me that many no longer believed God's Word, believed in Jesus' great work of salvation, the power of the cross and shed blood, and that people in the Church have come to the place of accepting sin as a natural part of their lives. I therefore wrote this series of messages and preached them, not only at my church but also at several camp meetings and revivals.

In 2018 I felt the Lord was asking me to leave my ministry of twenty-one years at Sturgis Evangelical Church and just open myself up to His leading and trust Him. After thirty-six years of pastoral work this was very difficult. I began to purchase a home in Sturgis, started working at a factory and am continuing to seek what God has for me next. This book is part of that "next."

These have been eye-opening days for me! I'm learning what it's like for our lay people to work in a worldly environment. What it is like to work fifty hours a week and have devotions and get to church. What it's like to get up at four in the morning so I can have a good devotional and prayer time. I'm learning what it's like to trust God when you have bills to pay and still be faithful in the giving of tithes and offerings, and the list goes on. But I want to say this: I want to apologize to all my people of my past congregations, revivals, and camp meetings, for not understanding what they are going through.

But the one consistent thing about the Church and the World is this: the doctrine of Calvinism— once saved, always saved— has taken its toll in both worlds. As I've lived and worked at the factory, I've learned that those working there that consider themselves Christians— all but one— live, cuss, smoke, just like everyone else. There is no distinguishing mark between them and the world that they live in. To be honest, I was amazed at how many consider themselves "Christian" when living in known and obvious sin.

I understand that God will be the final Judge and will judge people according to the light that they have. But I also understand that we are living in a "Christian" world that has forgotten that you cannot continue to choose darkness and be a part of the true Church. And what I saw going on outside the Church is the same as I saw in the Church, people willingly living lives in sin and still considering themselves Christians. What has happened? People are interpreting the Bible by their experience instead of allowing the Bible to dictate the experience they need to have.

Why? The doctrine of Calvinism— unconditional eternal security, that once you're saved you're always saved no matter what you do— is bearing its ultimate end in these last days in which we live. This is one of the reasons why, as Peter said, "…judgment must begin in the house of the God: and if it first begin in us, what shall the end be of them that obey not the gospel of God?" (I Peter 4:17) Jesus said, concerning the last days, "And because lawlessness will be increased, the love of many will grow cold" (Mathew 24:12). We see the fruition of this verse in our world today.

I'm writing this book as a reminder and warning to the Church of Jesus Christ that we need to come to grips again with the awfulness of sin and the power of salvation. That we must again distinguish between light and darkness. That God has called the Christian out of darkness into His wonderful light. That He has called us to holiness of heart and life. That we must be changed and transformed by the Gospel or we have not truly experienced the Gospel at all. And that, as Paul said, "Let every one that nameth the name of Christ depart from iniquity" (II Timothy 2:19).

I will share these messages pretty much as they were originally written and preached back in 2016. May the Lord help us in these days to steadfastly hold to His Word by the help and power of the Holy Spirit and in knowing that "My grace is sufficient for thee: for my strength is made perfect in weakness" (II Corinthians 12:9).

To clarify before the reading of this book: when I refer to "holiness" throughout much of this book I am talking about entire sanctification, the baptism of the Holy Ghost, a second definite work of grace in the Believer's heart, whereby the heart is cleansed of all inbred sin, original sin, the sinful nature, by the blood of Jesus, resulting in a pure heart, that comes by faith in Christ's provision on the cross.

—RODGER MOYER

Sturgis, Michigan

1
A Fresh Vision of What We are Up Against (Part 1)

1
A Fresh Vision of What We are Up Against (Part 1)

"For the wages of sin is death..." (Romans 6:23a)

ON JANUARY 18TH, 2016, AROUND 5:00 PM, God began to lay a series of messages upon my heart while I was waiting for a Wednesday night service. I'd been praying for meetings I was about to preach at Kentucky Mountain Bible College for about a month, with no clear direction, and then the Holy Spirit spoke and gave me the direction for which I was seeking.

The series was to be entitled *A Fresh Vision,* and the first two messages were to be "A Fresh Vision of What We Are Up Against." And what we are up against can be summed up in one word: SIN. The Scripture is familiar to us, Romans 6:23a; "For the wages of sin is death..." I begin these first couple of chapters talking about subjects I don't much like talking about— sin and hell. It's much easier to preach on grace and heaven. But sometimes the bad news makes the good news better.

I've become absolutely convinced, as I look at the "church" world today, that we have lost vision of the awfulness of sin and, more and more, we are buying into a Calvinistic view of salvation that treats sin lightly, and worse, wrongly. That we have lost vision of the Man whose name is "…Jesus; for He shall save His people *from* their sins" (Mathew 1:21, emphasis added).

We have lost the vision of the exceeding sinfulness of sin. And along with that we have lost the exceeding awfulness and sense of dread of hell. We cannot understand the power of grace, of God's mercy and love, of the power of the cross and shed blood, the hope of victorious living, as we should, until we see the dark side of things (sin and hell) clearly.

Therefore, we must have a fresh vision of sin in its fullness.

And dear friends, sin is an awful thing! It affects everything in this world, and it affects and infects every person who enters this world. And its awful influence is seen everywhere you look. It surrounds us, touches constantly our lives, and it is almost as prevalent as the air that we breathe. But unlike air it only brings death.

If you look at the newspaper, listen to the news with wars, political corruption and such, it is clear what sin causes in man and in this world. You can just take a walk-through any big-box store, or go to work, and the things you hear, the things you see, all influenced by sin! It literally surrounds us at every turn. When you just take the time to think through sin's total effect upon man and this world it is literally mind-boggling.

First, there is sin in general.

The Bible says in Romans 8:22 "…that the whole creation groaneth and travaileth in pain together until now." How much better if "the stones would immediately cry out" in praise of Jesus! But that's not our present reality.

What sin has done to nature, to God's creation, is an awful thing! We are told in Genesis that the ground is cursed.

And so we see the farmer out in the field putting up with drought, then too much rain, and disease. This is why a couple times a year over my old parsonage an airplane would fly over my house, too close, and spread chemicals to kill disease, to kill weeds (and most likely aid in killing me, too)! Then there are floods, tornadoes, earthquakes, and tsunamis! All that is the direct result of sin entering into this world.

Even the seasons of the year are a direct result of sin entering into this world. We were made to live forever, but we don't, do we? Why? One of the main reasons is because of the effects of sin on this world. We see it clearly in God's Word. Before the Fall of man and the changes of seasons, before the winter, summer, hot, cold, men lived to be seven hundred to nearly a thousand years of age. Then after the Flood, and now years later, we consider ourselves blessed to live ninety years. Our bodies were not made to live in that kind of true climate change. It's all a result of sin touching the things of this world.

Unbeknownst to most of us it's talked about more than anything else. We ask, "How are you today?" What are we asking? How are you doing up against the fact that you are slowly dying! Or we ask, "How's the weather?" We talk about the Fall of man and the Flood about every day.

But what about sin's effect on all people generally? There are sicknesses without number. Cancer, heart failure, flu, aids, arthritis, to mention of few. Just in the last few years I've had two surgeries and problems with my feet. It's all a result of sin in this world — not in us, but in this world in general.

Think about it. Picture in your mind all the lame people, all the diseased people, all the blind people, all the people who are going hungry, the bleeding, and the suffering around this world. If you could, picture all the hospital beds, all the prisons, all the graves from all over the world. It's all a result of sin in this world — not only in us, but in this world.

Then add to that all the people who are suffering from headaches, backaches, toothaches, leg aches, and heart-aches. And add to that every empty pulpit, every closed-down church, every persecuted soul, and you begin to get a picture of what sin has done to this world. If we could just get a vision to see sin for what it is and what it has done, and its existence, we would hate it just as we should and just like God does. If we could get a cure for this world today, we would, wouldn't we? I mean, even the world is constantly seeking a cure for all those things. What sin has done to the world is exceedingly sinful.

The Word of God is clear that someday there will be a cure for this world, for all this sin in general. It is called the Resurrection and a New Heaven and a New Earth "wherein dwelleth righteousness" (II Peter 3:13). And I say even so, come quickly Lord Jesus! Praise God, we are told in Revelation that there will be a day when "there shall be no more death, neither sorrow, neither crying, neither shall there be any more pain, for the former things are passed away" (Revelation 21:4). And to that I say Amen and amen! And all that will come to pass because there will be no more influence of sin upon our bodies or upon this world!

Secondly, let us get a fresh vision of what sin does in and through the lives of people.

Dear friends, as bad as all that sin has done to this world it still pales in comparison to what sin does to the personal lives of men, women, and children of this world. And we know it is a mess. Sin affects what people say, what people do, how people act, and what people think. And the truth of the matter is that when you see what sin does through people you see sin at it's worst. As bad as the world is, what people do is a matter of eternal consequence and destiny.

The Bible is clear about what sin causes people to do and we really don't even need our Bibles to see it. We can just look at life and see how exceedingly sinful sin is. Every murder, every lie, every divorce, every act of adultery, every molested child, every cuss word, every war, every act of illicit sex, every pornographic book, movie or Internet site, every kidnapping, every abortion, every act of homosexuality, every evil word of gossip, and every malicious slander comes because of sin.

Oh dear friends, sin is an exceedingly sinful thing! Every beaten child, every molested child, every abused wife, every rape, every ruined home, every alcoholic and drug addict, every bad thing in this life done and committed by people is because of sin. Sin is exceedingly sinful.

What sin has done through the lives of people is a tremendous thing and the Bible is clear, they that do such things shall not enter or inherit the kingdom of God. Sin is so awful that men even took the innocent Son of God Himself and hung Him on a cross! They beat Him, they lied about Him, they spit on Him, and they killed Him, a man who only went about doing good. We make no mistake about it, if Jesus' first coming was happening today they would do the very same thing. The Bible says that as time comes to a close on this earth that they will do that to His followers. It's happening in many parts of the world today. We also know this to be true because in the Last Days, when the two prophets of God come this world will put them to death and, in fact, celebrate it.

This is the battle we are in! Even the truth of God is going to be turned into a lie and they will call evil good and good evil. We see that all over the news today. A few years ago I preached against homosexuality at a Chris-

tian college and received from "Christians" hateful words
I would have never imagined.

Friends, the only cure is through the blood of Jesus,
through His grace, through His forgiveness, and through
His power to make us a new creation. Praise God, He
can and will set us free from that kind of living and thinking and we can be free indeed! But only Jesus can save
people from their sin. Sadly, it only gets worse. We not
only need our lives to be changed and our actions forgiven, we need a Deliverer, for thirdly we see…

What sin has done to the hearts of people.

All we have to do is look at all I just described as coming out of people and understand that what comes out of
man is because of what is in man. Jesus made it very clear
in Mathew 15:18- and 20 when He said, "But those things
which proceed out of the mouth come forth from the
heart; and they defile the man. For out of the heart proceed evil thoughts, murders, adulteries, fornications,
thefts, false witness, blasphemies: These are things which
defile a man…"

There is a root cause of the awfulness of sin in our lives
and it's the sin of the heart. It's described in Scripture as
the sinful nature, evil heart, a carnal mind. It's called by
theologians original sin and a bent toward sin. However,
it is described as a heart problem that every man, women,
and child on this earth is born with. Friends, if we are not
entirely sanctified and cleansed, given new purified hearts,
that seed of sin still dwells in us. Oh, let that grip us afresh!
It's this sinful heart of man in which we see our greatest
problem of all.

Listen, friends, we preach holiness and wholeness
for a reason. As long as that sinful nature is abiding in
us we have within us the capability to do all those outward sinful things I mentioned earlier. As Jesus said,
"for out of the heart" come these things. But it's not

just the things that come out; it's what resides in that sinful heart on its own. Lust, hatred, carnal anger, jealousies, selfishness and unbelief— it's all there! As Jeremiah said in Jeremiah 17:9, "the heart is deceitful above all things, and desperately wicked..." Oh, that the Lord will open our eyes afresh to the sinful nature and the ruin it causes in us and through us.

What I'm trying to do in this chapter is for you to see sin as God sees it. To hate sin as God hates it. To finish reading this chapter knowing afresh what sin is and what it does in and through us. I can't draw the picture of its evil well enough.

Secondly, I want us to leave this chapter hungering for Jesus, and looking to Jesus, for He is your and my and Everyman's only hope of being delivered from all those exceedingly sinful acts and the sinful nature within us.

Friends, it even gets worse than this. What so many preachers and theologians seem to forget and so many refuse to deal with is what is said in Romans 8:6, 7. When I was attending Vennard Bible College I had a class my senior year called The Doctrine of Holiness. The teacher, Dr. Robert Morris walked into the room on the first day of class and asked this question: "Why do we need to be entirely sanctified and cleansed of all sin?" After some silence he went on to quote Romans 8:7. Here are verses 6 and 7:

"For to be carnally minded is death; but to be spiritually minded is life and peace. Because the carnal mind is enmity against God: for it is not subject to the law of God, *neither indeed can be.*" (Emphasis added) In verse 7 we see the very root and exceeding sinfulness of sin— "the carnal mind is enmity against God: for it is not subject to the will of God, and neither indeed can be."

So here we have a God who is holy, righteous, and pure set against a nature which is unholy, unrighteous, and sinful. A nature that in its very essence is enmity, is opposed, is hostile toward God and His very nature. At this point every Christian on this earth should be screaming and crying out to God, "Get it out! Get it out, O God, and bless me with a clean heart."

I trust as you read this you understand. We have a God Who acts morally, with justice and goodness. He is set against this heart that moves and behaves immorally, unjustly, and selfishly. So that it is not only opposed to God in its nature but by the tendencies of its very behavior.

We have a God who is eternal, from everlasting to everlasting, Who is the source of all life. Set against the carnal mind that deteriorates us spiritually, decays us spiritually, and ultimately leads to death both spiritually and physically. Not only is this sinful nature opposed to God in nature, in its tendencies, but by its very destiny.

This sinful nature we are born with is opposed to God in every way. By its very nature it is going to oppose God viciously, bitterly, and utterly. It is enmity against God, which is a hostility and hatred. It is going to fight God with all it's worth as long as it finds life in us, for it is the very nature of Satan himself.

Oh, dear friends, there can be no unity here, no getting along, no working it out, no trying to smooth things over; it is God's enemy, our enemy, first, last, and always. To try to love God with all our heart and love our neighbor as ourselves, or pray for those who despitefully use us, and still have that kind of animosity abiding in us is a useless endeavor.

To say that we can please God consistently with that kind of nature in us is just plain scary. And if this is not the biggest problem in this world and in the unsanctified soul, I don't know what is. This is Calvinism at its worst. The idea that we have to live in this state of heart and mind is a doctrine that leaves us in spiritual failure constantly.

If our Savior, our Lord, our Jesus cannot defeat and deliver us from this problem we are utterly doomed to death, for by its very nature it will not stop fighting God. And by its nature it will lead us continually toward spiritual and eventually physical death. For to be carnally minded is death. Look at the words afresh: "...not subject to the law of God and neither indeed can be..." The sinful nature, like the devil himself, has no interest in God's law of love, of grace, of mercy, of reconciliation, or the holy life God wants us to live. It will always fight God, run from God, say No to God, and to any holy suggestion the Holy Spirit puts in your heart. It will always say No.

This is how exceedingly sinful sin is in the heart of man. It will always indulge in self-seeking, whether by pride, sex, power, position, fame, self-righteousness, or just plain old unbelief in the Word, the promises, and the salvation that can be found in Jesus.

Don't miss this: the sinful nature, the carnal mind, will never allow you to love God with all your heart, nor your neighbor as yourself. In the sinful state you will always tend and have a bent to fall short, because something within you always says No to the will of God. We can read and see the result in the next verse, in Romans 8:8, "So then they that are in the flesh [the sinful nature] cannot please God."

It is sin, both committed and actual, that we are up against. A clear vision of sin, its awfulness and utter sinfulness, and what it does to us and in us— that vision is what we are in danger of losing in these days where Calvinism has crept in so subtly and deeply into our churches. Even many of our "holiness" Churches are forgetting the need and the power of God, to undo all that the devil has done by the Son's blood and the Holy Spirit's power.

And yet, friends, it's even worse, as we'll deal with in the next chapter. But if you have found yourself weaken-

ing your stand on the awfulness of sin and its nature; if
you have allowed sin into your own life, or to settle in
your heart, why not let God deal with that today? There
is no reason to wait; there is no other answer; only Jesus.
His grace, His power, His love, His forgiveness, His cleansing, and His salvation— just Jesus! Look to Him!

2
A Fresh Vision of What We are Up Against (Part 2)

2
A Fresh Vision of What We are Up Against (Part 2)

"For the wages of sin is death..." (Romans 6:23a)

WE NEED, NOT ONLY A fresh vision of sin and what it has done to our world, our lives, and our hearts, but a fresh vision of death, for "the wages of sin is death." We need a fresh vision of the awfulness of hell, a final separation from God and everything that is good. We again must be reminded that sin's only mission is one of destruction, in nature and in us. Now, nature isn't moral. It doesn't have a choice. It's going to disappear, be burned up, and replaced someday with a newness in which only "dwelleth righteousness" (II Peter 3:13).

Sin in us is another story. Sin has two results and one end; physical death, spiritual death, leading us eventually to hell. Hell is an everlasting loss of holiness, of happiness, of heaven, and any hope of living with the Father, the Son, and the Holy Ghost. *Forever.* There will be no hope of meeting the saints of the ages, angels, or any of

our earthly family. We call that separation and place hell.
We don't have to imagine what hell will be like. We
can see it, we can read about it, in God's Word. Jesus Himself gives us quite a vivid picture of it through His teachings, but especially in Luke 16. Beginning at verse 23 we
read these words:

"And in hell he [the rich man] lift up his eyes, being
in torments, and seeth Abraham afar off, and Lazarus
in his bosom. And he cried and said, Father
Abraham, have mercy on me, and send Lazarus,
that he may dip the tip of his finger in water, and
cool my tongue; for I am tormented in this flame.

But Abraham said, Son, remember that thou in
thy lifetime receivedst thy good things, and likewise Lazarus evil things: but now he is comforted,
and thou art tormented. And beside all this, between us and you there is a great gulf fixed: so
that they which would pass from hence to you cannot; neither can they pass to us, that would come
from thence.

Then he said, I pray thee therefore, father, that
thou would send him to my father's house: For I
have five brethren; that he may testify unto them,
lest they also come into this place of torment.
Abraham saith unto him, They have Moses and the
prophets; let the hear them.

And he said, Nay, father Abraham: but if one went
unto them from the dead, they will repent. And
he said unto him, if they hear not Moses and the
prophets, neither will they be persuaded, though
one rose from the dead" (Luke 16:23-31 KJV).

If we could use one word to describe hell, a good word
would be "torment." And the first thing we see about that
torment is this:

It is a place of torment.

The Greek word used here for torment brings across the idea of the most awful, unbearable pain possible. It's a word that is stronger that being terrified. It's a word worse than tortured. This rich man, and all those that continue to live in sin, are going to be in torment day and night forever. This word also brings across the idea of extreme anguish of pain in both body and mind, touching both the physical and mental.

I don't know what the body will be like in hell, but I do know the suffering of the body will be worse than any kind of pain a person could possibly face on earth. We have all seen people in pain on this earth. We have all experienced physical pains, to one extent or another. It pales in comparison to what hell is going to be like. No earthy experience can do justice to what hell is going to be like.

This is a place of torment! It's worse than torture with bamboo shoots up the fingernails. It's worse than a constant drip of water on your forehead or chest. It is a torment, physical and mental, that will drive you to the brink of death and insanity, but you won't die nor go insane. You will want to die, you will want it to end, but it won't.

This is what the word *torment* means, and Jesus goes on to describe what makes it that kind of place. We need to remember that this description is not a re-creation of reality; this *is* the reality of hell. Let us not therefore push these thoughts aside. This is not virtual reality that we can get in and get out of whenever we want. This is a real place, this is forever, and this is a place for those who continue in their sin, for the wages of sin is this death.

The first torment will be the ability to see what you missed.

I will call this *Unrealized Joy*.

We see this in the words in verse 23, that "he lift up his eyes" and he saw Abraham and Lazarus. Friends, he could see the other side. He could see what he was missing. This is the first thing he saw. He didn't feel any peaceful feelings. There wasn't any joy or comfort. There weren't any friends or buddies to hang out with. No, he be eternally tormented by the fact that he missed his opportunity to go to heaven. This will be regret and torment at its greatest.

We do this all the time, don't we? What could have been or what I could have had, "if only!" If I knew that car would have been worth so much today, I would have never sold it. If I had known that piece of land was where they were going to build Disney World, I would have bought it.

I've thought about my own life as well. If I would have gotten to God earlier before all the drinking and drugs, what would my life have been like? How much better would my brain be operating? How many of my friends might still be alive? Not, saying to myself, "You dummy, why did you do that?" or "Why didn't you do that?" or "If I only knew then what I know now."

We live with things like that. "I could have, I should have, I came that close, but I missed the opportunity and it's gone." Friends, hell will be a place of far greater mental anguish than some old car! He looked up, being in torment, and saw heaven! What he missed and what he could now never have. He would live forever never having the peace and joy and life that heaven brings. Those that continue to live in sin "shall not inherit the Kingdom of God" (Galatians 5:21).

The second torment we can look at two different ways.

A place without water, of *Unquenchable Thirst,* or a place of flame, *Unquenchable Fire.*

It is a place where there is no water. The rich man was not asking for a glass of water, or even a thimbleful. He was just asking for a drop, a dip of the finger off someone else's hand. This man would spend eternity without one of life's most basic needs — water. You can live quite awhile if you have water. But if not, you can eat all you want but you won't last long.

In hell there is no liquid, no water available, but you won't die. You will live with that thirst and you add to that the torment of the flame, the unquenchable fire, and you have a picture of hell. I remember many times being thirsty or waking up thirsty. The mouth dry, the lips chapped, the throat so dry it was hard to swallow. I needed something to drink. Dear friends, this place called hell is worse than we can ever imagine.

The Bible uses other words to describe hell. It is described as the "lake of fire," a "lake of fire and brimstone," "everlasting fire," a "furnace of fire." I read once where John Wesley would ask people to put their finger in the flame of a candle to see if they could bear it just one minute. When they couldn't he would ask them, "Then how will you have your whole body plunged into the lake of fire and brimstone forever?"

I wish I could make this picture of hell as real to all of us as it should be. The torment of the thirst will not end. The torment of the fire will not end. The torment of seeing what you missed will never go away. You won't pass out; you will not die; turn up the temperature 500 degrees and it will not compare.

Look at this man. He just wanted a drop. He received none. No relief forever. He would beg for deliverance and healing, but there is none. We need to understand that there will be no one there to help you out, no friends to comfort you; there will be no fellowship and no time when you can say, "Well, I've had enough, guess I'll take a break now;" or, "I guess I'll repent now." No lessening of the punishment, no lessening of the anguish, and no time of release. You are in hell and that's it. Those that continue in their sin "shall not inherit the Kingdom of God."

The third torment is found in the word "remember."

There will be *Unwanted Memories*, tormenting memories. Remembering and regretting, remembering and regretting. You will remember the prayers from your parents as they prayed for your soul. You'll remember the calls of ministers, family and friends, as they urged you to find deliverance in Jesus. You'll remember the Holy Spirit tugging at your soul to leave your sin, and find forgiveness in Jesus, and how you put it off or said No. You'll remember how you chose the pleasures of sin, which were for a season, rather than the joy and peace of salvation and heaven, which are forever.

In this rich man's case Jesus points out something that most people don't like to hear. He says, "Remember that thou in thy lifetime receiveth thy good things, Lazarus evil, he is comforted, now you are tormented." One of my greatest concerns for us who live in America is that we are living too much for this earth. We are gathering goods, retirements, spending our lives working for things as if earth were supposed to be our heaven.

We struggle in America with this. Always trying to create for ourselves a utopia, a heaven on earth. We get so preoccupied with the things of earth making us happy, trying to free ourselves from any trouble or pain (we think money does that), to the point that we don't sacrifice ourselves, our money, and our comfort for the Kingdom of God, for Jesus' sake!

We too often are not setting our treasures in heaven. Oh, friends, let us keep our eyes fixed on a better city, a city not built with hands. Now here is this rich man remembering what a waste and how empty that is compared to eternity without heaven. Unwanted memories.

Then there is the torment of no escape, a "great gulf is fixed."

The *Uncrossable Gulf.*

It's over, it's too late, you cannot cross from one side to the other. The decisions have been made. You will live with your choices. There is no second chance. Hell, dear friends, is final. There is a great gulf fixed. There are no bridges. There is no annihilation, as some would teach. There is no purgatory, no moving from one place to the other by the prayers or gifts of people left on earth.

It is just simply over. The door to the ark of safety and salvation has been shut. It's done and knowing that will torment you more than we can even imagine.

The last torment will be the realization that you can do nothing about getting our loved ones one the right road to heaven and out of the place in which you find yourself—

Unanswered Prayer.

Your opportunity to lead souls to Jesus, to keep souls from the reality of hell, is over. One of the greatest evangelical calls in all the world is coming from the tormented souls of hell. One of the greatest concerns for souls of family and friends is occurring in hell. But in hell it's too late. There is no way for them to hear your concerns. Knowing that will torment you.

As I was thinking about these verses some people crossed my mind. Some of my own feelings for the lost, both at home and work, crossed my mind. The frustrations of watching family and friends and loved ones go in the wrong direction. The many "Christians" I know that have backslidden or have fallen into the lie that we can continue to sin and expect heaven. I pray burdened over souls almost every day. There is a mental anguish in that, many times crying.

Even that cannot compare to the tormented anguish

of the realization in hell. At least, here I can still tell some, share my testimony, and maybe reach a few with the saving Gospel found in Jesus.

But dear friends, if we could only hear the sounds of hell. In the midst of the screams of torment we would hear the tormented cries and the cry of unanswered prayers for family. *"Go tell my family! Go tell my friends!"*

They'd be telling us not to give up, to continue in the faith, make whatever sacrifices are needed. Nothing in this world is worth losing your soul over. I can imagine friends and family there saying, "Rodger, keep preaching. Rodger, don't give up. Rodger, don't fall back. Rodger, continue to follow holiness of heart and life! *Rodger, tell my family!"*

This is what we are up against if we don't experience Christ— the torment of hell. They won't hear you, it's not going to work, and your opportunity to help others is over. Jesus said it, "…if they hear not Moses and the prophets, neither will they be persuaded, though one rose from the dead." Jesus has risen from the dead, yet people will not listen.

As I close this chapter can I ask you, do you know Jesus as your personal Savior? Do you know beyond a shadow of a doubt that you are living for Him? Do you know that if you died today heaven would be your home? I feel in writing this chapter like the rich man. Someone shake them up. Cry to them. Plead with them! *Wake them up!*

One of my burning desires as I'm writing this book is that we will realize we are in dire straits in this world and we have lost the true meaning of Christianity. The awfulness of sin and the dread of hell for those who live continually in sin. Yes, I think in our present world Calvinism is to blame.

God has done everything in His power to keep you from sin and hell. He sent His only Son to die for you. He has given us His written Word. He has sent the Holy Spirit to convict us of sin, judgment, and righteousness. He is trying with all His heart to help us see and to make the right choices.

This is what we are up against— the danger of losing the sense of the awfulness of sin in this world, in our lives, and in our hearts. The danger of losing vision of the awfulness of hell for those who continue to live in sin. We have lost sight that God knows what we need and sent His Son to provide an answer, which we'll see in the rest of this book.

Dear friend, if you are involved in some secret sin, please, don't even take a chance. You don't want to go to this place called hell, and you need Jesus to save you from this destiny. You need Him today!

3
A Fresh Vision of the Savior

3

A Fresh Vision of the Savior

"For the wages of sin is death; but the gift of God is eternal life through Jesus Christ our Lord." (Romans 6:23)

NOW FOR SOME GOOD NEWS! The Gospel! I trust the first two chapters showed us how desperately we need a Savior. That we saw the exceeding sinfulness of sin and the awfulness of hell. That we now see the exceeding greatness of our Savior. I begin by quoting several Scriptures.

John 1:29— "Behold the Lamb of God, which taketh away the sin of the world."

Colossians 1:14— "In whom [Christ] we have redemption through his blood, even the forgiveness of sins..."

II Corinthians 5:17— "Therefore, if anyone *is* in Christ, *he is* a new creation; old things have passed away; behold, all things have become new." (NKJV)

I John 1:7— "But if we walk in the light, as he is in the light, we have fellowship one with another, and the blood of Jesus Christ his Son cleanseth us from all sin."

Revelation 1:5— Jesus, "who is the faithful witness, and

the first begotten of the dead, and the prince of the kings of the earth. Unto him that loved us, and washed us from our sins in his own blood…"

Our focus verse, "…but the gift of God is eternal life through Jesus Christ our Lord."

We could go on and on quoting Scripture after Scripture of what a great Savior we have in Jesus, for His salvation touches, overcomes, and conquers all that sin has done in this world, to people, and to our hearts! Amen and Amen! Hallelujah, what a Savior! Thank you, Jesus! Out of all the people in this world from the beginning of time, Jesus is the one Person we need! Out of all thing things of this world, His salvation is the one thing we need!

Yet we know, that people in this world seemingly "need" everything but Jesus. They think they "need" a newer car, they "need" a bigger home, they "need" a better retirement, they "need" an easy life, they "need" a new boyfriend, girlfriend, husband, or wife, and they especially "need" money, money, and more money. Sadly, so many don't have the one Person and thing they really need— Jesus and His salvation, a Savior from sins, from sin, and from hell.

If you would take a walk through a store and just ask people, "What do you really need in life?" how many would answer, "Jesus"? Yes, it is Jesus we need more than anything in the day in which we are living. There is crime, war, confusion, and political corruption all around us. Jesus is the Answer. Jesus is "the Way, the Truth, and the Life." He alone can deliver us, deliver this world, and He alone is the Answer.

There are a lot of good things in the Bible. There is instruction about how to live. There is instruction about how to raise your children. There is instruction on how marriage and the home are supposed to function. There is instruction about prayer. There is instruction about everything we need to really know about life.

But the real message is found in the few words from the angel who said, "There is born in the city of David, a Savior!" Everything, friends, from Genesis to Revelation points to that one Person and to that one event.

We need a Savior, a Deliverer, and a Rescuer; One Who saves us out of this mess of sin that leads to death. The word *Savior* implies that we have something we need desperately to be saved from. If not, God Himself would not have come to deal with it. He would not have sent His only Begotten Son to give His life to deal with it. He would not have sent the Holy Spirit to convict of sin, judgment, and righteousness. We have a serious problem that has to be dealt with— sin, sinfulness, and hell.

We should be praising God that Jesus has come to be "the gift of God." Jesus came to deal with all three of these issues. He came to take care of something we cannot handle and man himself has no cure for. He came to deal with something we cannot defeat, something we cannot control— the sin problem that will keep us out of heaven and from the presence of God. Sin is the only thing that can keep us from heaven. It must be dealt with.

Friends, any religion, any Gospel, any doctrine, that doesn't take care of the whole problem of sin and deliver us from hell is not good enough. Some have settled for that— not me. Some religions mess with sin, some cover it up, some make God blind to it, some play games with it or even just forget about it, but we need a Savior, a Rescuer, a Deliverer, One Who saves from all sin.

Years ago, I was swimming in the Sacramento river. That river is known for its undercurrents. Before I knew it, I was taken under and came up, out of breath, about twenty-five feet down the river from where I was. I panicked! I began trying to swim back to where I had been and was getting nowhere.

Then I heard my brother John yelling at me from the bank, "Don't swim against the current, swim sideways to the shore." I feel like my brother may have saved my life that day. But what if he would have stood and said, "Just stay in the water; don't worry about it," or just declared I was on the shore but left me in the water? I would have drowned. I would not have been delivered, rescued, or saved.

We need a Savior Who delivers us *from* sin, not *in it*. To leave me where I was is to leave me in death, for "the wages of sin is death." I meet a lot of people in the world and Church world today who want to talk about their sin problem. You know what they are looking for? They are looking for someone or something that will save them from the results of sin but not from the sin itself. They want a "get out of jail free" card.

In their heart they still love darkness more than light. They want out of hell but want to continue in sin. They need a Savior *from it* but are settling to continue to live *in it*. They want the nature of sin, which leads to death, not to change, instead of a work of God in their life that transforms their behavior and changes their nature. They don't want to become "a new creation" with "old things passed away."

They want out of hell, but they don't want to live for Jesus, serve Jesus, give their life to Jesus, and leave their sins behind by His power and grace at work in their lives. Friends, that cannot be done, for the nature of sin never changes; its one outcome is eternal death.

So, I bring to you with all my heart, and all the praise I can muster in my being, the Answer, Jesus, Savior, and Rescuer! Who must and can deliver us!

Jesus delivers us from the acts of sin.

He must, or He is not truly a Savior at all.
We remember some of those sins from chapter one —

murder, lying, adultery, homosexuality, lying, pornography, malicious slander, abuse, and the list went on and on. We need to be saved from those sins and from the power that sin can have in and upon our lives, because "they which do such things shall not inherit the kingdom of God."

Every day we live in sin it gets a tighter grip and hold over our lives. We can't get rid of it to save our souls. Sins have become habits and addictions. We need a Savior, a Rescuer, Someone Who can save us and deliver us from those sins. Someone had to come to help us. The Bible is clear, "all have sinned and come short of the glory of God."

I remember one of my terrible sins was smoking. I'm not going to debate whether smoking is or is not a sin to you. I know God told me it was for me. It began as a game on a date but soon I was addicted to those things. At times I would get under conviction about it, feel guilty about it, and literally sick of them. I knew it was wrong and those things were killing me both spiritually and physically.

Sometimes I would throw the pack of cigarettes out the window of my car and just decide to quit. A few days later I'd be back at it again and I couldn't quit those things to save my soul. I couldn't do it. Maybe you have some other problem, like pornography, lying, or drinking.

But, thank God, there is a Savior! I got down on my knees, poured my heart out to God, and confessed my sins. As a result, not only did God deliver me from my smoking, but all my sins — the drugs, the swearing, the lying, the stealing — and He saved me, rescued me, and delivered me from all that. Why? Because He is the Savior!

If you are living in any known sin, two things you need to know. One, you are headed to death and hell unless you get to God, for the wages of sin is death. Two, you can get to God through Jesus Christ the Savior. He is well able to deliver you and rescue you from your sins just as He did me.

The drunkard can be saved from his drinking. The liar from his lying. The curser from his cursing. The sexual addict from his sex addiction. Jesus can save anyone instantly from whatever He has convicted them of.

I can guarantee, that if you will repent, and get hold of Jesus by faith, God can work a miracle in your life so that you can live free from all that used to bind you. I know, because I've experienced it. Do not let anyone or any false doctrine say He can't or that we can't help living in sin. No, there is a Savior, a Deliverer, and a Rescuer!

The Bible is clear, when Jesus does His work, we are a "new creation." Amen! Not act like one, not try to be different by our own power, but literally a new creation in Christ, with old things passed away and all things becoming new. This happens because you have truly been rescued by the Rescuer, delivered by the Deliverer, and saved by the Savior!

Praise God, I have found it true! Have you? Have you heard the words of Jesus in your soul, "Son, Daughter, your sins are forgiven and you are set free." This deliverance is not a process but an instantaneous work of the Son of God Who, along with the Holy Spirit, is powerful to deliver. If He can raise the dead and heal the sick, He can definitely deliver you from your sins.

The "gift of God is eternal life" through Jesus because we have been delivered from the "acts of sin." With John, (from I John chapter three, in my own words) "Don't let anyone deceive you about this, those who are born of God do not continue in their sins. If they do, they are of the devil. This was the whole purpose the Son of God has come, that He might destroy the works of the devil."

The Answer? Jesus only! We need not only a Savior Who

delivers us from the "acts of sin" but from what sin has done to our very hearts and nature. So, I once again bring to you with all my heart, and all the praise I can muster in my being, the Answer— Jesus, Savior, and Rescuer! He must and can deliver us!

Jesus delivers from the attitudes of sin.

He must, or He is not truly a Savior at all.

We remember some of those other sins from chapter one as well— lust, carnal anger, jealousies, pride, unbelief, selfishness, and enmity against God. There remains in the born-again believer something in the heart, the very being of who we are, that wants sin and demands its own way.

I am not now talking about smoking, drinking, lying, or any other outward sins. Those are to be taken care of when we are saved by the Savior. We are speaking about a heart that has something in it that fights God's full will and whole will in our lives; something in the heart that will not freely submit to Jesus. It is a bent in our nature that is enmity against God and not subject to the will and law of God.

We may never take a drink, we may never cuss a swear word, we may never smoke a cigarette, but yet there is still sinfulness in the heart that when God demands something of you it will say No. God says to love Him with all your heart and you can't because self is first. God says we are to love our neighbor as ourselves, and we find ourselves getting bitter or angry at them. God says to pray for those who despitefully use you, to turn the other cheek, but you can't. Something in your heart won't permit it; something that says No to God continually.

It can be something as simple as going to church like we should. It can be giving our tithes and offerings like we should. It can be giving to a missionary, but the love of money in us won't allow it. The rich young ruler couldn't do it. When God asks for all, the heart will argue and say No.

Friends, we need a Savior, a Rescuer, a Deliverer from that attitude of sin. Please understand, I'm not being overly dramatic about this. There will be a lot of people in hell who have never smoked, cussed, or whatever, but they were never able to give their hearts to God. We need someone to save us and cleanse us from that "no," that "enmity" in our hearts. Why? Because to be "carnally minded is death."

Oh, friend, we have an Answer in Jesus! He is the Savior, the Rescuer, and Deliverer. *He is the One.* He shed His blood, and the Bible tells us in I John 1:7 that His blood cleanseth us from *all* sin. The Bible says we can have pure hearts. I thank God and praise God, I know this to be true in my own life.

I know we can love God with all our heart. I know we can love our neighbors as ourselves. I know I can pray for those who despitefully use me. I know we can readily obey God and love to have it so. There is a peace of heart that bears witness to this work of Christ, that you are living as He has commanded.

I know we can love our enemies and pray for them, and love to have it so! I can love church, love prayer, and love giving sacrificially, and love to have it so. I can have a heart that is set free to love God and serve God rather than serving sin, self, or this world. Yes, the acts of sin can be forgiven. Yes, and the heart of sin can be cleansed, purified, and made new. Jesus can do both through His shed blood and work of the Holy Spirit. What sin has done to our lives can be defeated. *What sin has done in our hearts can be cleansed.* Friend, do you know the fullness of His work in your heart today?

Yet there is more. We need a Savior from the acts of sin, from the attitudes and nature of sin , but also one Who can cure this sinful world.

Jesus can deliver us from the atmosphere and results of sin—

—Or we don't have a Savior at all. "I know this earth, O God, don't leave me here to live in this world as it is." Remember some of this from chapters one and two? All the sadness of this earth? Some of the greatest words in the Book of Revelation are these: "It shall be no more." No more sorrow. No more pain. No more death. No more sickness. No more sin. No more devil! No more corrupt world! *No more!*

No more heartbreaks, heartaches, headaches, leg aches, or sore throats. No more disease, no more war, no more death, no more sin and sinfulness and sinful world to deal with. *No more.* Why? Because we have a Savior, a Rescuer, and a Deliverer.

And hell? We don't have to worry about that, either, as we live in Him. He is life and hell is death. He is love and hell is hate. He is hope and hell is despair. *Someday, dear friends, we'll be free from not only the effects of sin on us, but also this fallen world.* Amen!

Yes, the wages of sin, in continual act and nature, are death, but the "gift of God is eternal life through Christ Jesus our Lord." I will say it from my heart again, "Hallelujah, what a Savior!" He is the Savior, Rescuer, and Deliverer!

He can save us and deliver us from the acts of sin. He can save us and cleanse us from the heart attitudes of sin, purifying the heart. Then, when we have experienced those two great works of His grace, then someday (and in no other way but through His salvation experienced in us), we'll be delivered and rescued from the very atmosphere of sin with a new heaven and a new earth. We'll be delivered from the result of sin, death and hell, and have eternal life. Heaven! Hallelujah, what a Savior!

4
A Fresh Vision of Biblical Repentance

4
A Fresh Vision of Biblical Repentance

"...except ye repent, ye shall all likewise perish."
(Luke 12:3, 5)

WE NEED A FRESH VISION OF the first work of grace, of
repentance, of what it means to be born again. What
I've been seeing more and more of in these days is
that we are calling people to holiness of heart, to
be entirely sanctified, who haven't met the condition of initial sanctification. They haven't been
saved from their sins.

More and more I am dealing with people in the church
who are beginning to seek God for entire sanctification
when they are still dealing with sins that should have been
taken care of in the first work of grace. So many times, I
have gone down to help someone at the altar seeking a
clean heart and end up dealing with the issues of sins.

As one young man said, "I believe I've been sanctified
but I keep looking at pornography on the internet." I
had to tell that young man, "Listen, you're not even saved
yet if you're still doing that." People are still lying, cheating, and involved in sins, and we seem to be trying to get

people entirely sanctified who are still living in their tres-
passes and sins.

This lets us know how much Calvinism, the "once
saved always saved" doctrine, has invaded the mind and
hearts of so many people these days. It is a message that
has us uniting with Satan, who basically said to Eve, "You
can sin and not die." No, as we learn from I John 3:7-10,
he that continues to commit sin is of the devil (verse 8).

A lot of what the church world is facing today, with its
apathy and laziness toward sin, is due to this doctrine. It
has led us to a day where people are half-heartedly seeking "first the Kingdom of God." It has led to a lack of
seeking holiness of heart, preaching holiness of heart, and
experiencing it. These things are the result of a lack of
genuine repentance being preached and experienced in
the souls of people. You cannot experience the second
work of grace without experiencing the first.

We are trying to get a holy Church, "without spot or
wrinkle," without first having people truly getting saved
and forgiven. They are not truly getting saved and experiencing God's forgiveness because they are not meeting
the condition, that is, a call for repentance.

We can look at the compromise in the Church in the
world today. It is full of the World. There is a lack of love
for God, a lack of love for His Church, a lack of love for
one another, a lack of love for a lost world. Today, more
than ever, drinking and smoking, even homosexuality,
are being accepted commonly by the Church. Sports,
shopping, working around the house are taking prece-
dent over worship of the Lord.

Slowly the clear teachings of God's Word against abortion, homosexuality, and other obvious sins is no longer
stood for by the Church world in general. I had a former
pastor of mine when I was in Bible college tell me about a
movie he saw. I said, "Doesn't that have nudity in it?"
His answer was, "Yes, but it was done in good taste."

Friends, we are Christians, or we are not. We have become no different from the World in too many areas.

I truly believe the general Church world is living in the time of the great apostasy, the great falling away from the faith. We are living in a day where there is a strong delusion in the Church, that we can continue in sin and be God's people; days the Bible describes as coming upon the Church before the Second Coming of Christ.

What I share in this chapter is very heavy upon my heart for the lost and the deceived. We must have a fresh vision of what it takes to be born again, to be called "Christian," and what it takes is genuine Biblical repentance.

The Bible has a lot to say about repentance. It was the first message from John the Baptist. He said, "Repent, for the Kingdom of God is at hand." It was the first message of Jesus. Jesus, in our text, preached it more strongly— repent or perish. Jesus is leaving no room for doubt, for error, or for an either-or situation.

I attended a church recently where the pastor closed with a "repeat after me" salvation prayer, and how they were now saved, but said nothing about the need to repent of their sins. Peter preached repentance on the Day of Pentecost. Paul preached it strongly. We need to know what repentance means, as if our souls depended upon it, because they do.

What is *repentance?* Accepting Christ as your Savior? Turning over a new leaf? Trying harder to change your ways? A change of mind? Reformation? It includes some of those elements in some form or another, but the truth is that most people in the Church today can't give you a Biblical answer to that question. We look then to God's Word for a right definition because no other definition will do when our souls are at stake.

We need also to step back and look at ourselves, and ask the question, "Have I truly repented of my sins and been born again?" Not just trying harder, not just presuming on the grace of God, not just feeling better about myself because I've made some changes, but have I truly repented?

Let me give you a definition of Biblical repentance and then go over it in greater detail. "Biblical repentance is being so convicted of sin by the Holy Spirit, that a soul, in godly sorrow and remorse over the sins, with God's help, confesses those sins, turns away from those sins, and turns to Christ by faith for what He did on the cross to forgive them."

I've mentioned many things in that definition. One thing God does, and several things we must do. God convicts and then I react one of two ways. I may just say No and shrug it off and continue to live in my sins. Or I can react positively to the merciful voice of the Spirit. While conviction may not seem like a blessing it is one of the greatest ways God shows love and mercy toward us. It is showing we are on a path of sin that leads to hell, and that there is a Savior to save us from our sins Who has paved a path toward heaven for us.

In the positive aspect, we react with a sense of remorse and godly sorrow for our sins. We then confess that we have sinned and are determined with God's help to turn away from those sins. Lastly, we believe God for the saving and forgiving grace of Jesus to be poured out on us by our faith in His sacrifice on Calvary. Again, the Holy Spirit will help us.

We need to remember that repentance itself does not save; God does. Repentance simply makes us acceptable to God because we have fulfilled the basic requirement that He has asked for. He said, "...except ye repent, ye shall all likewise perish." Repentance and faith in Jesus are the only things that will keep us from dying for our sins and going to that place called hell.

Let us work through the areas in a little more detail.

God's work of conviction

We must be shown our sin and drawn to Jesus. In our sinful condition we'll never seek God on our own. We must be convicted of our sins and shown that there is an answer in Jesus. This is one of the purposes of the Holy Spirit, as we have mentioned, to convict the world of sin, judgment, and righteousness. John 16:9 — "Of sin, because they believe not on me."

This just makes sense. You can't confess what you don't know. The Holy Spirit's work is vital to us, and we need to pray for this conviction to be made manifest in this world. The Holy Spirit shows us our sins. He will do that faithfully so that every person will stand before God without excuse. He is alive and well and doing that work today. Again, this is mercy at its best.

Every soul in this world can know God in good saving grace because of His work. He will do His work, He will convict the soul, He will bear witness of truth to our heart, and let us know exactly where we stand with God in light of the convicting power of the Holy Spirit. We will repent or make excuse. We will either walk in the light or continue to live in darkness.

Let it be known that the devil will put in our minds all the excuses in the world. Oh, that people would face this conviction honestly. It comes down to this: we will react positively, or we will perish. Friends, what our soul is before God is what it really is, nothing more and nothing less. We need to face that.

We need to understand, once again, that we can live free from committing known sin in our lives through the grace of Jesus and power of the Holy Spirit. We can say No to the devil and his temptations. We can obey God and defeat the devil and be pleasing in God's sight. If we will obey the Holy Spirit's promptings upon our heart and repent of our sins God will give us grace and power to live right. The Holy Spirit's conviction is vital to us, so that we can know we need to repent of our sins and that there is a Savior Who saves us from our sins. Don't lose the vision of a Savior.

This leaves us back to our original question: What is repentance? What is our part in this "so great salvation"? God has done His part by convicting us of sin and showing us the Savior. What must be our response if we don't want to perish? Repentance!

Repentance includes godly sorrow for your sins.

That sounds simple, but is it Biblical? Yes, for we read in II Corinthians 7:10, "For godly sorrow worketh repentance to salvation..." David said in Psalm 51:17, "...a broken and a contrite heart, O God, thou wilt not despise."

We are talking about godly sorrow, not just being sorry because I got caught doing something— sorry because I got caught cheating on my taxes, cheating on a test, caught watching pornography, committing adultery, or whatever.

This is realizing what you have done against God. Judas repented and then hung himself. He had a sorrow that led to death. Peter cried out to God for his sin and found forgiveness and renewal. I have experienced both worldly sorrow and godly sorrow in my own life.

Years ago, around 1980 when I was heavily involved in drugs, I had a "bad trip" on LSD. I won't get into details, but I thought I was going to lose my mind. During that night I remember begging the Lord to get me through that experience and I would follow Him. He helped me through, but I continued to go down my own path of sin. This was worldly sorrow.

In 1981 I got down on my knees with my wife and we asked God to forgive us, and to save us. We promised to make restitution, to leave any known sin, and to walk with Him. We were truly sorry for what we had done in our lives, but also sorry for what we did to God. We were saved because we had godly sorrow, which led to repentance.

This repentance is more than just admitting you're a sinner. About everyone I've ever met does that! Sadly, even many who call themselves "Christians." I heard one man say at a church service we were all "sinning saints." What utter nonsense! Biblical repentance involves a painful remorse in your soul that you have sinned against a pure and loving God, Who sent His Son to die for you.

This comes when we have seen our sin as the exceedingly sinful thing that it is. No true repentance will occur until your heart is broken over your sins— godly sorrow. There is no such thing as just saying a "sinner's prayer" or just "accept" Jesus and you'll be saved. Repentance is deep heart-brokenness over sin.

This is a godly sorrow that falls on its face before God over sin and asks in brokenness and humility, "Lord, would you accept me?" This "softness" of what it means to be a Christian is a curse to the true Gospel. From many pulpits you never hear anything about truly repenting anymore.

The result is that there are more and more people calling themselves Christians without any definite transformation in their lives because of repentance. They have never realized the awfulness of sin and the power of what Christ had to go through for their soul's sake. Many in the Church are still without Christ and living without victory over sin. We have lost the mighty outpouring of God working in people's lives.

I clearly remember when the Holy Spirit began to show me my sins. It was like a pain that wouldn't go away. Conviction was gnawing at my insides. I couldn't relax, take it easy, because I had a need only God could take care of. I couldn't get right with God until I was truly sorry for the sins I had committed.

It was more than just being tired of that kind of life. It was more than just trying something new. It was not just wanting to get to heaven. It was more than being sorry for what the drugs and drinking were doing in ruining my life. I was sorry that I had sinned against Him! That I had sinned against myself, my wife, and my heritage. I didn't blame anyone but myself for my sins. When I reached that desperation, I could truly repent. Why? Because "godly sorrow worketh repentance."

I know it's not always easy to make that choice. There is the pressure of friends who don't want you to live a Christian life. There is the habit of doing some of those things. There are other "Christians" who will tell you, "After all, we all sin; you're okay, God loves you." There is the devil himself sitting on your shoulder whispering in your ear, "Don't worry about it, you're good enough. You can continue in sin and get to heaven. God wouldn't sent you to hell."

I remember when I was in high school and group of Christians were waiting across the street to hand out tracts and talk to people about getting saved. The lady that talked to me was a pastor's wife and asked me if I was saved. I said, "I used to be but I'm not now." She responded, "Oh, son, if you were once saved you still are," trying to assure me that I was unconditionally eternally secure. I'm thankful I was raised in a holiness home and that I could not be deceived by that lie. I told her, "Lady, I know I was once saved, but I am not now!" I then walked away. I knew how I was living, and it wasn't like Jesus at all.

The devil will say things like, "Just wait until tomorrow and you'll feel differently." He is right about that, you probably will if you wait. If you don't obey the Holy Spirit while He is speaking to you, if you don't seek Him while He can be found, if you don't call upon Him while He is near, you will walk away and most likely forget about it, and the devil couldn't be more pleased.

I don't know how many times as a young man I walked out of church services feeling the conviction of God on my soul, knowing that I wasn't right, knowing I was choosing sin and hell. Thinking to myself, "If I can just make it through that last stanza of the altar song. If I can get that first step out the door it'll go away and everything will be okay."

I actually thought, in my sinful state, I was accomplishing something good by doing that, and not realizing that what I was doing was losing out on everything God had for me; that I was losing my soul; that I was hardening my heart; that I was taking another step toward hell; that I was taking another step away from heaven.

I trust the point is clear. There must be godly sorrow for it to work repentance unto salvation. If you have been convicted to the point of godly sorrow, what's next?

Repentance includes confession and a turning away from your sins.

Is that Biblical? Yes! I John 1:9 says that "If we confess our sins, He is faithful and just to forgive us our sins..." Confession simply means that you agree with all that the Holy Spirit has convicted you of. It's admitting that you are guilty. It's saying, "God, you are right, I am a sinner and You are my only hope." We don't blame others. We don't blame our circumstances. We blame no one and nothing but ourselves. It's like the old song, "Not my father, not my mother, not my sister, not my brother, but it's me O Lord, standing in the need of prayer."

There must also be an inward determination that all that He has convicted you of will stop. Is that Biblical? Yes! Jesus told the adulterous woman, "Go, and sin no more" (John 8:11). We are told in II Timothy 2:19, "...let everyone that nameth the name of Christ depart from iniquity." For some it may be something you have to start, especially if you're backslidden. I was called to preach when I was six years old at Orchards Camp in Washington state. To be saved, not only did I need to leave those sins the Holy Spirit convicted me of, but fulfill God's will in becoming a minister.

The point I'm making is that God will not accept any repentance that does not include confession. He will not accept any confession that does not include a determination to quit the sins that you have been convicted of. Let us not be deceived (I John 3:7). In my own words, I John 3:9— "Whoever is born of God does not continue in his sins, for His seed remains in him; and he cannot continue to sin, because he is born of God."

This means if (like in my case) you were convicted of smoking, the smoking stops. And drinking, it stops! And drugs, it stops. And stealing, it stops. And pornography, it stops. I was convicted of all these sins and they stopped the very day I repented. God changed me. He moved upon me. He poured out His grace upon me. Instantaneously, in all the light I had, *I was made a new creation in Christ and old things were passed away!* Amen!

I started going to Sunday School and church the very next Sunday. I started tithing, putting God first and walking in all the light I had. I went from swearing to preaching. From serving and living for the devil to serving and living for God. Instantly, I went from pursuing sin and this world to pursuing holiness of heart and life and a home called heaven. It was a radical change. The places I went, the people I hung out with, all changed. Why? Because I repented. I was broken over my sins, I confessed my sins, and was determined to leave them and serve God.

Repentance is more than a heart broken over your sins. It is also a heart broken away from those sins.

When you truly repent you enter a never-ending war against sin in your life and the devil. I trust this kind of repentance speaks to your own testimony; that there has been sorrow for sin, confession of sin, and a turning away from sin.

I will not speak of restitution except to say you'll make things right as far as possible.

One last point.

Repentance includes faith in God to forgive you because of what Jesus did on the cross.

Is this Biblical? Yes! Ephesians 2:8, "For by grace are ye saved through faith; and that not of yourselves: it is the gift of God." Paul said there must be "repentance toward God, *and* faith toward our Lord Jesus Christ" (Acts 20:21, emphasis added).

This does not mean, "Just take it by faith." It is not faith in faith. There is no power in faith unless that faith is placed in God. This is not emotions or feelings, although there may be some of that. This is laying hold on the promises of God that, upon repentance, He will forgive you from your sins because of what Jesus did on Calvary. He will respond to your godly sorrow and confession, as He said He would be "faithful and just to forgive us our sins."

We praise God because this is the invitation of God to every sinner in the world, that we repent and be saved. Please remember our text, "except ye repent, ye shall all likewise perish."

This is all foundational to begin the Christian life. You cannot look for answers to prayer. You can't look for God's sanctifying grace. You cannot look for His blessing upon you. David was clear in Psalm 66:18 that "if I regard iniquity in my heart, the Lord will not hear me."

One last word of encouragement. The Holy Spirit not only is faithful to convict you of your sins, but He will help you confess them, turn from them, trust in Jesus, and help you to live a wonderful Christian life in the eyes of the Father. God is good!

5
A Fresh Vision of God's Incredible Love
(And Our Incredible Love for Him)

5
A Fresh Vision of God's Incredible Love (And Our Incredible Love for Him)

I John 3:1-10

THERE ARE TWO WAYS people tend to look at God's love and grace when it comes to salvation. The most popular position in the Church world is that God's grace covers, looks beyond, and basically ignores our sins. We are told we sin because we are human, and all that God can do is look at us through the covering of Christ. God no longer sees us but sees Christ's righteousness. (We'll deal with some of this in a later chapter)

The other position is one that, with Paul, says "His grace is sufficient" enough for all our need. That His grace is strong and powerful, and not only brings forgiveness, but also can deliver us from our sins and change our lives. A faith in God that says, "God, if you can raise the dead, heal the blind, You can deliver me from my sins and help me to live a godly life for Your glory."

In the last chapter I came back many times to I John

chapter 3. It's a very strong passage and one that those who believe in a sinning religion struggle with greatly. I read from one commentator these words: "This is a very difficult passage." That just depends upon your theology. I want to deal with this passage from the aspect of God's love and our love. For every action there is a reaction.

There is no greater subject on this earth that we can discuss that's greater than God's love. For if God loves us it means that He is not far off. You run to those things or people you love. If God loves us it means He is not unreachable. You want to be near those you love. If God loves us it means He is deeply concerned about us. You care for those you love. And friends, *God loves us.*

If God really loves us, that means He will bring into our lives everything we need to get to heaven. He has done that, praise His name! He has given us His Son, His Spirit, the gift of His written Word, and the family of God to help us through. Friends, *oh, how God loves us.*

If God really, *really*, loves us, then He will not let us go easily or without a fight for our souls. He will be faithful to warn us, discipline us, and mold us just like any good parent. He will give us every opportunity, by His grace, to be the kind of people we need to be to reach heaven. Oh, friends, *how God loves us.*

If God really, *really*, REALLY, loves us, He will care for us and pour out His strength upon us. He will help us through trials. He will help us through temptations. He will walk by our side through the difficulties of living in a sinful world. He will be there, praise His name! *Oh, friends, how God loves us.*

More deeply, He will provide a way that we might be saved from our sins that lead to death. He will give us new pure hearts because the sinful heart is enmity against Him and leads to death. *Oh, friends, how He loves us.*

If God really, *really*, REALLY, *REALLY*, loves us He will demonstrate that love to us. He has done that through the giving of His Son. The Son has done that through His cross, His shed blood, and bearing upon His body the sin of the world. His Spirit has done that through the conviction of that which leads to death. His Spirit has done that in showing us there is a Savior. His Spirit has done that through, upon repentance, applying the blood. His Spirit has done that by entering our lives and being our Guide. *Oh, friends, how God loves us.*

If God loves us in all those ways and in many more ways, He desires a reaction to that love. He desires us to respond to Him in the same way He responded to us, by giving our lives back to Him and loving Him with all our heart. *Oh, friends, how He loves us. Oh, friends, how we ought to love Him!*

God loves us and we need to respond, receive, and experience His incredible love and return that love to Him. I John 4:19 has it right: "We love Him, because He first loved us." Amen!

I can show my wife and children all the love in the world but if they don't acknowledge it, receive it, or in their heart of hearts experience how much I love them— beyond the flowers, gifts, and words— then they haven't experienced my love at all. They must experience in their hearts, my heart. Yes, the love is still there but it must be experienced.

Anyone who genuinely experiences and receives the love of someone else will return it, especially when it's God's love we are talking about. If we truly experience in our heart of hearts the love of God, we will return it. We will have a loving relationship with Him. God's love is so incredibly great, incredibly intimate, incredibly infinite, incredibly immeasurable, so wonderful, so full of mercy and grace, that if you know that love in your heart, and experience that love in your life, that love will be shown by your actions, reactions, and in every area of your life.

It's a love and life based in your thankfulness for all He has done for and in you.

If our lives are not changed, we've yet missed the experience of His incredible love to us. This is beyond attending church, singing hymns and choruses to this loving God. John comes to us in this passage and gives us some clear instruction how to identify our own experience with God, to see if we have experienced the love of God, or not.

Have we experienced God's incredible love? (I John 3:1)

This is the first logical question. The first verse of I John chapter 3 is one of my favorite verses in the entire Word of God. I quote it all the time. I think about it almost daily— the great privilege it is to be called the "sons of God."

I don't know if you get this when you read this verse, but every time I read it or quote it, it comes to me with absolute wonder, glory, and amazement. "Behold [look, see], what manner of love the Father hath bestowed [or poured out] upon us [me], that we [I] should be called the sons [the children] of God[!]"

This is an amazing thing. This is God's incredible love to us. We were born into this world sinful. That sinful nature, enticed by the devil, has driven all of us to sin and come short of the glory of God. We were children of sin. Children of the devil. Living under the devil's grip, under his rule, under his leadership. We were lost and undone.

We had a nature in us that was absolute enmity against God; not subject to the will of God nor would ever be. We sinned, we rebelled, and we ignored God. We disobeyed God, rejected God, and denied Him. We lived doing our own thing, living and loving our own lives, and we were headed to a devil's hell. We've all been like this in some form or another.

But, "Behold," John says. "Look at this," John says. Look and behold what God has done in His love. He has reached out to *me*. He moved upon *me*. He spoke to *me*. Think about what David said in Psalm 8, "What is man that He is even mindful of us?" Now here He is doing this incredible thing, showing this incredible love.

He received me. He changed me. *Made me part of His family.* Have you experienced, and in your heart of hearts, known this incredible love of God? I'm not talking about just an acknowledgement, a frilly sentimental thing that God loves me — as Richard Taylor called it, "warm fuzzies."

We are talking about an experience of heart glory and reality. A genuine heart experience; a genuine transforming grace that literally floods your soul with the knowledge. "Look, behold, I'm now a child of God. I've been born again. I've been bought with a price. While I was yet a sinner Christ died for me. I've experienced His love and grace. *Old things are passed away, all things are new!* I'm SAVED!"

If you have had such an experience with God, through His Son and Spirit, like John you know you are a child of the Creator, the Supreme Being of the universe. So much so you cry out with Paul, "Abba, Father," or with Thomas, "My Lord and my God."

You understand that this love of God is so amazing that it took me, a rebellious sinner, who deserved only the wrath of God, and made me His son. God took me, a person who didn't want anything to do with Him, and reached out to me in love and mercy and saved me. He took me out of the devil's family and made me part of His. And now, He lives in my heart!

This is experiencing the incredible love of God. You live every day in thanks to Him for that incredible mercy and love. Oh, friend, let us not forget, or ever leave, our first love. John says here, "The World doesn't know us because they don't know Him." Many people don't know Him at all. We find this even in many churches. They haven't experienced the incredible life-changing love of the Savior.

They don't understand the excitement over going to church rather than staying home to watch a football game. They don't understand the excitement of giving to the Lord's work even when you're low on money. They don't understand why you love your devotions and prayer time enough to get up a little early to start your day. They don't understand why you support missionaries and pray for them. They don't understand us because they don't know Him in His incredible, life-changing love. They don't know Who He is, what He has done, that just makes us from our hearts love Him. We love Him because He first loved us.

That's all just from the first verse. Beginning in I John 3:2 we begin to see that we have hope of some even greater (if that's possible) things to come. God's sons have some things to look forward to for "it doth not yet appear what we shall be." Then John says the most incredible thing: "...we shall be like Him"! In holiness; in righteousness; in a glorified body; *in eternal heaven.* No more temptations, no more pains, no more dying, and no more living in a sin-filled world! *No more.* This is all part of God's incredible love to us.

Do these truths move you? Are they moving your life today? How *should* they move us? To answer that question, we share another thought.

Are you experiencing the incentive that comes from experiencing God's incredible love? (I John 3:2,3)

Remember we are answering the question, "How do you know if you really love God?" First, you know because you have experienced His incredible love. He saved *even me.* You have a testimony. The only real proof of that love of God is by your heart's desires. We can talk all we want. We can sing all we want. We can claim all we want. But we know we've experienced His incredible love when our heart incentive is to be holy. This incredible incentive directs our hearts, directs our minds and, as John puts it in verse 3, "And every man that hath this hope in him purifieth himself, even as he is pure."

We are living in a world, and a Church world, that have forgotten these words, this pursuit of holiness of heart and life. The word *purifieth* is a verb of continual action. It's the continuous aspect of sanctification that begins the moment you've experienced His incredible love.

I'm not asking was there a time in your life when you wanted to avoid sin and sinful things. I'm asking if that's your heart's desire daily; that there is this inward incentive to have your actions, your attitudes, and your activities, glorify His name. This phrase used by John here speaks of "an anxious striving by all means" to keep yourself pure, unmixed with sin, both in actions and attitudes. Therefore, we pray, we worship, we commune and fellowship with God, we listen and read His Word, we go to church, and we pursue holiness of heart and life. Why? Because as John says, the love of God and the hope of heaven stirs us to.

This is no longer of conviction of sin but a conviction of want and desire. When you know the love of God, the mercy of God, you are stirred to holiness of heart and life. This is what Paul was referring to in Romans 12:1, 2 when he said, "...present your bodies a living sacrifice..." — why? His answer: because of "the mercies of God."

People who have experienced God's incredible love crave holiness. When you have a hope to be in heaven with a holy God, holy angels, in a holy city, for the whole of eternity, it will drive you to holy living.

We have experienced God's incredible love. That is

proved by this inward incentive, not only to avoid sin, but to be like Him. Then comes a third question.

Is this experience of God's love, and this incentive to be holy, indicated by your life? (I John 3:4-10)

Experiencing God's incredible love and the incentive to be holy brings with it the indication of both those experiences. The fruit of repentance, the fruit of knowing the love of God and the desire to be holy, is to leave all *known* sin. This indication always follows the true experience of God's love and grace.

John is very powerful here. If we live in sin, if we are continuing to do the things and living a life we know we ought not to live, it is a clear sign we do not yet know the love of God in our hearts and have the incentive to be holy. It's not being indicated by the way we live.

I want to be clear at this point; no person, no matter who they are, no matter what they claim, no matter what their past experience may have been, no matter what "gifts" they seem to have, can continue to live in *known* sin and keep grace upon their hearts. To continue to live in *known* sin is not an indication of salvation, but an indication that you are still part of the devil's family.

Living in sin is living like the devil, not Jesus. Jesus is our Lord, our God, and our example. To be like Him is always the goal. Purifying ourself, even as He is pure.

I know the battle we are up against these days, with all the television preachers and popular book writers continually telling us we can't help but sin— the lie of Calvinism. I challenge you to read God's Word, to believe your Bible. God's Word says that "whosoever abideth in Him sinneth not" (verse 6) and to continue in sin is to have "not seen Him, neither known Him."

Friend, as I've already written, we need a Savior, a Rescuer, a Deliverer from our sins, and Jesus is the answer. Through Jesus, through the Spirit, there is ample provision for victory over temptation, for the Bible says He "will with the temptation also make a way to escape" (I Corinthians 10:13). By His grace we don't have to sin, for His grace is sufficient for all our need (see II Corinthians 12:9).

The Bible says "we are more than conquerors through Him that loved us" (Romans 8:37). Adam Clarke put it this way: "Jesus came into this world to destroy the power, pardon the guilt, and cleanse the pollution of sin. He was born, suffered, and died for this purpose, and He can and will accomplish what He came to do" (from verse 8).

Friend, Jesus is our Provision. Don't cut His love and power short. He is the perfect provision and in Him we have all we need. As John the Baptist said, He is the Lamb of God that taketh away the sin of the world. As John makes clear in our text verses, when we are "in Him" we don't continue to sin. There is no continued sinful lifestyle.

It must grieve God, the Father, the Son, and the Holy Ghost, to see people who claim to know Him and love Him continue to live in sin, and believe that after all God has done He can't provide an answer for us. Oh, how God loves us!

The only proof that we truly abide in Him, and are saved right now, is if we have turned away from the practice of known sin out of our love for Him. That's the indication God is looking for and His Word teaches.

John tells us in verse 7 not to be deceived about this. Don't be deceived by anyone who might tell us we can't be saved from knowingly sinning in this life. Don't be deceived that because you were once saved you can't lose your relationship and experience with God. The Bible is clear. "Let no man deceive you" (I John 3:7).

To experience God's incredible love is an amazing event that puts within you a desire to live a holy life, to have a holy heart, and that desire is indicated by being free from a sinning lifestyle. You can claim to experience the first two, His love and have that inward incentive, but does your life bear that out?

"Behold, what manner of love the Father hath bestowed upon us, that we should be called the sons of God."

6
A Fresh Vision of the Purpose of the Cross for the Believer

6
A Fresh Vision of the Purpose of the Cross for the Believer

"Sanctify them through thy truth: thy word is truth. As thou hast sent me into the world, even so have I also sent them into the world. And for their sakes I sanctify myself, that they also might be sanctified through the truth. Neither pray I for these alone, but for them also which shall believe on me through their word..." (John 17:17-20)

THE CHURCH HAS LOST the main focus of why Christ came to this earth. A lot of things can be mentioned for why He came. He came to be our supreme example of Christian living. He was an outstanding example of holy living and holy dying. He was our supreme example of love, grace, faith, and of steadfastness. Every one of us ought to follow His example in all those areas with all our heart.

His main purpose was not just to show us that He was the Messiah, the Son of God. Yes, He proved that He was God and that God was in Him and He in God. He didn't come just to show us His power by healing the blind, loosing the lips of the mute, bringing sight to the blind, or even raise the dead. He did all that and He can still do it today, praise His name! But none of those things were His main purpose.

Neither was it His main purpose for us to look at the cross and say, "Man, that's what self-sacrifice is all about. That's what doing the will of God is all about." Yes, it is that, a supreme example of the self-sacrificing spirit that God wants from all of us. We are to take up our cross, deny ourselves, and follow Him. But that wasn't His main purpose.

All these things are true and important. But they fall woefully sort of showing us the depth of the human need and the infinitely glorious provision God has made to meet that human need. God's main purpose in the gift of His Son Jesus coming to this earth was a redemptive purpose, first, last, and always. For He is the same yesterday, today, and forever.

God gave His Son that sinful people might be reached in their sinfulness and shame, and lifted out of the depths of that sin and shame into the freedom of knowing forgiveness through His grace and shed blood. Moreover, our Lord's life and death were redemptive in the sense that they make possible for the Believer a complete recovery and restoration to the moral image of God that was lost through the Fall.

Jesus came to provide for the sinner pardon from his outward transgressions. Jesus also came for the Believer, to cleanse him from his inward corruption. This prayer of Jesus in John 17 clearly shows us the ultimately purpose for which He came for the Believer ("I pray not for the world," vs. 9). A Believer is one who has repented, turned from their sins toward God, and has been born again. It is one who has experienced God's incredible love. Let's look at this passage a little deeper.

This prayer gives us a clear expression of God's divine purpose.

We see the outward expression of Jesus' heart desire for His disciples in two words: "Sanctify them" (verse 17). In other words, *Make them holy; make them clean; cleanse them from every trace of selfishness, pride, and unbelief. Father, make them one in heart and in purpose.* For those who identify the word *sanctify* with only one aspect of its definition, separation, Jesus had already said, "They are not of the world, even as I am not of the world" (verse 16). This prayer is for something deeper.

This is powerful because it is expressing in prayer, before His own Father, His whole desire for them as He leaves this world. This is one of the few times in the Gospels where the whole content of Jesus' prayer is shared with us. Often in the Gospels we see Him pray, or in prayer, or tell the disciples how to pray, like in the Lord's Prayer, but here, while He is addressing the Father, we get to overhear His prayer. When we read this there ought to be an awe in our heart and a humbleness of blessing. We are in the presence of a praying Man, in this case the Savior of the world and the Son of God.

Because of Who He is we ought to pay earnest attention to His prayer, and heed its content just as earnestly. This is our interceding Savior praying His deepest desire for His people to the heart of His Father. Let us not forget who He is praying for. Verse 9 says, "...but for them which Thou hast given me," and verse 20 says, "...but for them also which shall believe on Me through their word." That's us!

This petition is on behalf of those who have believed and placed their faith in the Lord Jesus; those who have become His earnest followers. The disciples had left their old lives behind, their old jobs behind, and even their families. They had become men of faith who had experienced His incredible love, and they had been born again. As Jesus said in Luke 10:20, "your names are written in heaven."

Now Jesus, the Master, the Teacher, the Messiah, and Savior is addressing His Father for the deeper need of their hearts, a need for inward purity. Remember, that prayer is for us today, for those "which shall believed on Me through their word." This prayer is just as valid for us today as it was for the Eleven, approximately 2020 years ago.

Furthermore, this prayer is significant because of the burden of this request. "Sanctify them through Thy truth." Let us never lose sight of how deep this prayer is in Jesus' heart for His people. These were His friends, His disciples, the ones who would build His Church. Jesus was not trifling with the matter. He wasn't leaving it up for debate. From His heart of hearts to His heavenly Father, He prays for His people, "Sanctify them!" Do this work in them. O Father, how they need this!

He is saying, Don't send them out; don't let them try to build the Church; don't let them face this work of ministry, the persecution, the trials, the emotional and physical battles, before they have this work done in them. He's not praying for gifts or power, but for one thing: sanctify, cleanse, purify their hearts.

Let us not lose the sense of the timing of this prayer. Jesus is about to go to the cross. The disciples were about to be left behind to preach the Gospel. This was an urgent prayer for them and for us today. Think of it. Right now, Jesus is praying, interceding for us as we face our ministry and our world, "Father sanctify them, purify them, and fill them." Why? The ultimate purpose is revealed in verse 23, "that the world may know."

There is a second thought we need to see here.

We see Jesus' own dedication to make this prayer a reality in his people.

This desire is revealed in verse 19, "And for their sakes I sanctify myself." The Lord is dedicating, giving, setting Himself aside for this sacred purpose in the hearts of His people. This work of entire sanctification of His people is that important to Him and thus, that important to us.

What is Jesus' sanctification? In what respect is it different from ours? This dedication goes deep and further back, for in a sense this dedication began when He agreed to leave Heaven for our souls at the request of His Father.

At the time He agreed to assume a human form and identify Himself with this world, its humanity, among sinful people, would involve the deepest humiliation of all. He gave up heaven for earth, having no infirmities to a body full of infirmity. There would be crying, hurting, and dying. This was greatly understood by Paul when in wrote in Philippians 2:5-8:

> "Let this mind be in you, which was also in Christ Jesus: Who, being in the form of God, thought it not robbery to be equal with God: But made himself of no reputation, and took upon him the form of a servant, and was made in the likeness of men: And being found in fashion as a man, he humbled himself, and became obedient unto death, even the death of the cross." (KJV)

Another version of the Bible puts it this way:

> "Let this same disposition be in you which was in Christ Jesus. Although from the beginning He had the nature of God he did not reckon His equality with God as a treasure to be tightly grasped. No, He stripped Himself of His glory, and took on the nature

of a bondservant by becoming a man like other men. And being recognized as truly human, He humbled Himself and even stooped to die; yes, to die on a cross." (WNT)

His dedication continued in life, as He was born into a humble home in a stable, poorer than most of His day. He lived in a little town called Nazareth. That is where He lived and worked and assisted His carpenter father. The King of Kings and Lord of Lords was, as the Bible says, obedient to His parents.

His total dedication and consecration were also seen in His ministry. We of today sometimes think we have it bad. It wasn't easy for Jesus to minister when even at times His very family turned on Him. It wasn't easy to deal with the stubbornness, and often foolishness, of the men He had appointed to be His disciples and apostles and to build His Church.

It wasn't easy to deal with the Pharisees, the Scribes, and the Sadducees when they continued to hound Him, argue with Him, and criticize Him. It was hard when the religious authorities of that day accused Him of being of the devil. These people were after Him day and night, literally thirsting for His death, and swaying people constantly away from Him with their words.

Even the good things He did wasn't easy for Him. It wasn't easy for Jesus when He was drained of His resources of compassion and healing and virtue, by the crowds who thronged around Him. Yet He lived and faced all these things without complaint, being completely devoted to His Father's will.

But supremely and ultimately this dedication and consecration is seen, in the context of this prayer, in His facing of the cross. This was what was foremost on Jesus' mind at the time of this prayer. While all the other dedications were good and powerful, an example for us to follow, this dedication to the cross was fully and only laid upon Him. This was His work to do.

The cross was clearly before Him and the hour was ready to come. He had to go to the cross to be faithful to His Father's will and for His love of the world and His love for His people, the Church. He had to die. He had to shed His blood. He had to bear the sin of the world. And it was a horrible death.

This is what Jesus was praying when He said, "I sanctify Myself." He was very conscious of all the implications that waited at the hands of those who were sending Him to the cross. He was conscious of the cost to His own body and to His own heart. He was conscious of the sin of the world He would bear upon His sinless being.

So why that kind of consecration and dedication? What was the purpose of it all? We see it again in verse 19, "...that they also might be sanctified through the truth." It is good to note that Jesus' sanctification differs from ours in a great way. Jesus had no inward corruption, no carnal nature, and no original sin to be cleansed from His heart, while we, as born-again Believers, still do.

Jesus had no lack of the fullness of the Holy Spirit and power, while we must be cleansed of our sinful hearts so the Holy Spirit can have us fully. Jesus' sanctification was a sacrificial and redemptive devotion of Himself from the Incarnation to the cross, to do the Father's will in order that we might be fully recovered in heart from the pollution of sin, which Jesus never had to deal with. Furthermore, our cleansing must be experienced so that our purpose can be sacrificial and redemptive toward this world, in the sense of living and witnessing in His power. Jesus' blood was our only answer.

Our sanctification would never have been possible without His consecration to the cross. It takes the Believer's own consecration and cross to experience the cleansing that He provided through His blood. Just as clearly as forgiveness and pardon were provided by the cross for the unbeliever, so also is the cleansing of the heart provided by His blood for the Believer.

It says in Ephesians 5:25, 26, "Husbands, love your wives, even as Christ also loved the Church, and gave Himself for it..." Why? "That He might sanctify and cleanse it with the washing of water by the word." The purpose of His sanctification (consecration) was for our sanctification (cleansing).

The provision was Himself, and through His blood He made possible the complete restoration of man to his pre-fallen moral condition. While still being human we can be free from sin, praise His name! By first being saved and forgiven, which the Disciples had experienced, as all Believers do. Then, by being sanctified by that very same blood so He can restore His moral image in us. Amen! Which the Disciples experienced at Pentecost and what all Believers need to experience.

We have discussed the purpose and provision; one last thought we before we end this chapter.

The personal question and application.

Jesus made it clear when He said, *I'm not just praying for the disciples but also for those who believe in their word.* If we are born again, if we have experienced God's incredible love through repentance of our sins, Jesus is praying for us right now, at the right hand of the Father, "Sanctify them."

Have you experienced the answer to this prayer in your own soul? We can nullify His prayer, His will, and the fullness for which He shed His blood, by refusing to walk in the light of His prayer and provision. God's holy will and Jesus' wonderful prayer can be nullified by the human will. Despite a perfect and full provision in the cross of Christ, it still requires the consent of the human will to make this our own Christian experience.

Yes, the atoning and cleansing blood of Christ can be rejected, and God's full redemptive provision and purpose thwarted, as though Jesus never died to provide it. Don't lose the thought of Jesus' words, *For this purpose I sanctify myself, that is, consecrate myself, in one great decisive act, to do my Father's will and go to the cross and shed my blood.* Why? *For the further purpose that my disciples who have been saved, whom you have given Me, might be cleansed of all sin.*

Friend, God has opened up before us the floodgates of His power, of His grace, of His Son's blood, of the availability of the fullness of the Holy Spirit, of a complete deliverance from all sin through the suffering of His Son, the shedding of His blood, and of His death and resurrection.

In this prayer is revealed the only answer to be delivered from every hateful and evil poison that pollutes our hearts and streams into our lives. Is this prayer a reality in you?

Thus, comes the question, have you, as a born-again Believer, had this prayer of Jesus, honestly and truly answered for you in the experience of your heart and life? Can you testify to it?

This was Jesus' last prayer for His people before He went to the cross. It was the most important thing on His mind for them to experience before they were left to build His Church. We know, in their case, they tarried in Jerusalem, prayed in the Upper Room, and experienced two wonderful things. First, in Acts 2:4, "And they were all filled with the Holy Ghost." Secondly in Acts 15:9, "purifying their hearts by faith."

Friend, just like the first work of saving grace, if you were the only one on this earth, He still would have died for this second work of grace, this cleansing, for you.

In today's Church we are trying to disciple people to build God's Church, yet this work of entire sanctification is most often, if not always, neglected in that preparation. This prayer reveals what was foremost upon Jesus' heart for His Disciples and us, the greatest preparation needed to build His Church, the cleansing fullness of His Holy Spirit. Oh, how foolish we have become. We neglect this truth even when it comes directly from our Savior Jesus Christ, in prayer and in provision. May God help us to experience, teach, and preach this wonderful work of Jesus! It is still the most needed thing to build His Church!

7
A Fresh Vision of the Enemies of Holiness (Part 1)

7

A Fresh Vision of the Enemies of Holiness (Part 1)

"O foolish Galatians, who hath bewitched you, that ye should not obey the truth, before whose eyes Jesus Christ hath been evidently set forth, crucified among you? This only would I learn of you, Received ye the Spirit by the works of the law, or by the hearing of faith? Are ye so foolish? having begun in the Spirit, are ye now made perfect by the flesh?" (Galatians 3:1-3)

WHAT I WANT TO DO IN the next three chapters is to make us aware of some of the areas of doctrinal confusion that we face in our day, errors that take us away from the simplicity of faith in Jesus. I want to do my best to show you that holiness, that of heart and as a way of life, is not just a matter of my opinion. It's not just the opinion of the Nazarene Church, or the Wesleyan Church, or the Evangelical Church, or any other denominations.

I realize in our day of political correctness in the world

that if you take a stand for or against something, you are considered a bigot. If you stand against homosexuality, abortion, Islam, you are considered unloving, a homophobe, a fool.

There has also become a political correctness that has entered the Church world. If you come out, as I am in this book, and say that without holiness (in life and heart) no man shall see the Lord (Hebrews 12:14), and you are dogmatic about it, and you say you are going to have to go this way or you're not going, especially in religion you are also branded as a bigot, as unloving, hard, and you yourself are considered not holy.

I want you to know there is a lot of error in the Church world today. I want you to know there is only one way to heaven and it's a highway, and as Isaiah 35:8 says, "…it shall be called The way of holiness…" Because it is found by faith in Jesus, we don't have to know it theologically. We don't have to understand every detail doctrinally about it. But in your heart, you must have it, and in your life, you must live it. It is just that simple, as again, Hebrews 12:14 makes so clear.

Truth is truth! And truth is that which is according to fact. The Bible did not create truth, it simply reveals to us what is already true. Truth existed before anything was ever written down. It's important that we know truth so that nothing can sway us away from it. That keeps us from moving into areas of compromising what we find in God's Word.

Every sermon I've ever preached comes with the weight of that thought. I will give an account to God for what I have done with His Word. Even in writing this book, I have a sense of fear and trembling, that I will answer to God. Truth is big stuff.

The devil is our Public Enemy Number One when it comes truth. The devil is very interested in truth. He is very interested in holiness. Not that we understand it or experience it, but that we miss it. He is interested in it because it destroys his most effective work in our hearts. The greatest evil ever done to humanity was what the devil did back in the Garden of Eden when he caused man to sin against God and thus corrupted man's moral nature.

We need to also remember the devil is not playing games with us. He has one purpose, and that one purpose is to send every one of us to hell forever. That is his one unchanging goal for every person in this world. It's his goal for you, for me, and it was for Jesus, too. He is no friend. The greatest way for him to get that done was to plant in our natures a bent toward sin. Every Christian denomination agrees with that point.

He planted in our natures by deception, and by man's choice, a nature that would agree with his way of thinking. We call it carnality, depravity, and theologically it's called original sin. The Bible uses terms like "an evil heart of unbelief", the "sinful nature." David said he was "shapen in iniquity; and in sin did my mother conceive me" (Psalm 51:5).

The Bible teaches we are all born sinful. The devil did such a masterful job that, other than Christ, every person is born with this sinful nature. Because of that sinful nature all of us have sinned and are coming short of the glory of God (Romans 3:23). As the hymn "A Child of the King" says in the third verse, second phrase, "a sinner by choice and an alien by birth."

This sinful nature, except for the fact of prevenient grace and the strivings of the Holy Spirit with our souls, would lead us all to death and hell without a chance in the world. A reminder: Romans 8:7 says that "the carnal mind is enmity against God: for it is not subject to the law of God, [and here's the kicker] neither indeed can be." This cannot be subdued or held under; it is a war to the death. There is in this sinful nature a hatred of God the Father, the Son, and the Holy Ghost. There is no getting along with each other.

Back in the Garden of Eden Adam and Eve made a 180-degree turn. They were created by God to be holy, and they were. They were made to love God with all their heart, and they did. They were made to walk with God, and they did that, too. What a fellowship they had with their God!

Then the enemy of their souls came, and they obeyed his will instead of God's will concerning the fruit of the tree. At that moment, they headed away from God just as fast as they could. They hid from His presence, the very presence they had previously longed for. This is a lesson for all of us. When we begin to hide ourselves "from the presence of the Lord," beware! When we don't want to be in church, when we don't want to have devotions, *beware.*

Friends, if not for the mercy of God and the future atonement of Christ, they would have gone into oblivion. If carnality, this sinful nature, had its logical end, if it went unchecked, we would all be beyond the realm of saving. Why? Because left to itself it is enmity against God. We would be fighting Him all our lives.

If God would not have put a floor under us called prevenient grace, and a consciousness in our heart to speak to us by the help of the Holy Ghost, we wouldn't have a chance, not one of us.

John says in his Gospel and in his letters, *These things are written that you might believe* (John 20:31; I John 5:13). What God has done repeatedly in the Bible, and by the help of His Holy Spirit, is to try to get us to open our hearts and to knock down the wall of resistance of sin and unbelief. He is trying to get us to open the door (the Door is Jesus), and let Him in by faith. That's the whole reason for the Book we call the Bible.

God wants us to once again love Him with all our

hearts. As Paul told Timothy, *This is the end of the com-mandment, love out of a pure heart.* A love toward God, a love toward others, a love toward our enemies, and a proper love toward self; this is what God wants to renew in us.

The devil is doing everything he can to keep us from experiencing that kind of love again, or to keep us fo-cused on other things so as to distract us from seeking this love. He's doing all he can. He is doing all he can to keep us from our own personal crucifixion, just as he tempted Christ. He is trying to keep us from having a faith in what only the blood of Christ can do. He has never changed.

This is what he tried with Christ: He tempts Him to make bread out of stone. Why? To step out of trusting His Father to meet all His needs, to live by works instead of by faith. He tempts us the very same way. If we pray a little more, if we go to church a little more, if we just try to work our way to heaven, that'll be good. That's what it means to live by works instead of by faith. But it would bypass the cross.

Then the devil tempts Jesus to jump off the pinnacle of the temple. Why? To do something spectacular so that people will come, things will be exciting, and they will follow Him for that reason. We are tempted the same way. Speak in tongues, concentrate on healing, miracles, something more exciting than just the Gos-pel. That is to live by emotionalism, and it sucks people in; but it bypasses the cross. It is not living by faith in Christ.

Then the devil tempts Jesus by offering Him the world. Why? To bypass the cross. He tempts us the very same way. Concentrate on riches, power, retirement, and the things of this world— after all, it's God's blessing. As it was for Christ, it is for us. The devil is always trying to get us to bypass the cross. We could spend a whole chapter on these thoughts as they concern us and concern the thinking of today's Church world.

We live in a day of much doctrinal instability. We live in a day when people want to bypass the cross, both Christ's and theirs. There are so many preachers, both men and women, so many books written that sound so good, that many people get easily side-tracked. As the Bible says, they follow every "wind of doctrine." We are living in a day when so many can't even discern truth from error, right from wrong, and what to believe and not to believe. Many are so confused it's very difficult to reach them at all. A day when Jesus alone is no longer the Answer.

Many people, because they don't read their Bibles as they should, or hear the Word of God preached as they should, fall prey to every new error that is preached. I heard this saying one time, taken from a church sign, "Something that is almost right, is still wrong." Friends, that's true. The devil therefore tries to focus on error and get us to stop reading God's Word to sidetrack us. But he has one goal in mind — to keep you from the cross and from your cross.

Being carnal or sinful in nature makes us susceptible to that. Here come the Mormons, or the Jehovah's Witnesses, and those who focus on outward signs or things, and many people are getting swindled and swayed from the truth. You have those who focus on tongues, or works, or eternal security. The one thing all error has in common (and the devil knows this), is to keep us from experiencing the full work of Christ in our hearts that cleanses from all sin and delivers us.

Without the cleansing blood you are always left to works. You go to the Christian bookstore and you see hundreds of books on "working" on sins or the sinful nature. "How to deal with pride." "How to deal with anger." "How to deal with bitterness." It never ends. Always leading us to a manmade process and always leaving out the instantaneous power of faith in the blood of Jesus Christ.

These books remind me of some of the false priests and prophets of the Old Testament during Jeremiah's day. "...They have healed the hurt of the daughter of my people slightly, saying, Peace, peace; when there is no peace" (Jeremiah 8:11).

There is nothing Satan fears more than that a Believer be made clean, whole, free from sin, sanctified wholly and filled with the Holy Spirit. That they be made "meet for the Master's use" and just sold out to God. His whole effort toward the Christian is to blind them to God's provision of a complete cleansing in this life from all sin in the heart by faith through the blood of Jesus.

With the devil's help and the devil's ally within, the carnal man is always fooled into going about to establish His own righteousness. Paul said it well in Romans 10:3, 4— "For they being ignorant of God's righteousness, and going about to establish their own righteousness, have not submitted themselves unto the righteousness of God. For Christ is the end of the law for righteousness to every one that believeth."

The Bible is very clear and so I'm constantly amazed. We have the Jews and the Amish who are trying to receive righteousness and heaven by works. I'm amazed at the number of Catholic and Protestant churches who have fallen into the very same trap, trying to be what God wants us to be, holy in heart and life, by works.

There is a Great Physician. His name is Jesus. Whenever we move in any way away from Him, we end up in the hands of another physician, the devil or one of his physician's assistants.

What I want to begin in this chapter and the next, is to make you aware of some of the other "doctors" out there who are offering a cure for what only Jesus, the Great

Physician, can do. "Physicians" who take or distract us away from the cleansing blood of Jesus; "physicians" that are "healing the hurt slightly" when Jesus' blood is able to meet the need of heart cleansing by faith.

Years ago, I read a book called *The Double Cure* by a man whose name was Martin Knapp. The idea of using false doctors is not mine, but most of the content is. If we don't understand the substitutes for the blood of Jesus, we will eventually end up discouraged or give up in our quest for a holy heart.

For our foundation we turn to Galatians 3:1-3, where we see the first substitute "doctor" for heart holiness. I know some of these verses may apply to being saved as well, but Paul, and hopefully I, are talking to Christian people who need to go on to holiness of heart. So our first doctor is one we've mentioned.

Dr. Works

I am constantly amazed at the Church as a whole. I am amazed that the very same people who would argue with you over being saved by faith and not by works. We are saved by grace through faith lest we should find something to boast about, or somehow lift ourselves up and say, "Look what I accomplished; look how I found the favor of God; look what I did to be saved."

The whole Church world would argue that point, including me. We can't save ourselves; we know that. Here is what is amazing to me: many of those very same people, when you talk about being cleansed from all sin, about being entirely sanctified, purified, and clean in heart, will say, "O, well, that's by some other method other than instantaneously by faith in the blood of Jesus." Or that we can't have clean hearts at all. Why?

Jesus has the power to wash away all our sins. Jesus has the power to give us new life. Jesus has the power to make us new creations. Jesus has the power, through His

Spirit, to keep us from habitual sin in our life. But that same Jesus, that same blood, does not have the power to clean up our hearts and cleanse our moral nature. Why? It's amazing!

Paul felt a little of some of that thought process when you move on to Galatians 3:4— "Have you suffered so many things in vain?" In other words, Haven't you learned anything yet? Weren't you saved by grace through faith? The Bible teaches us repeatedly we can be cleansed in heart. The fact that this cleansing is His call, His will, and His provision is taught throughout Scripture.

The Bible talks to us about a clean heart, a pure heart, and a holy heart. All these words that clearly bring you to the conclusion that there is nothing left in the heart that is unholy or unclean. Can a heart be clean and dirty at the same time? Can a heart be pure and impure at the same time? Jesus said in Mathew 5:8, "Blessed are [present tense] the pure in heart..."

Only Jesus can make the heart clean. Only Jesus' blood can cleanse us from all sin. The devil knows this, so he is about the business continually of telling good Christian souls that there is another answer, another physician. The doctor he was offering the Galatians, and so many churches and Christians today, is Doctor Works— that somehow the cleansing of the heart is not by faith but by works of the flesh.

Here is the thing about any substitute concerning God's work in our hearts: they always fall woefully short of the real thing. They never meet or accomplish the need. Remember, this was the very problem of the Pharisees and Sadducees of Jesus' day.

They had all their rules. You can't walk too far on the Sabbath. You can't lift anything on the Sabbath. Even if Jesus heals and tells you to take up your mat and go home, nope, that's working on the Sabbath and you can't do that.

The very things that were not to be done, that weren't supposed to be works, turned those things into works of salvation. Nothing has changed over the years. Instead of allowing Jesus to come and cleanse our hearts by faith, we come to the conclusion that if I don't do this or I do that, the cleansing will come. No, it is only by our faith in the shed blood of Jesus. Remember, this sinful nature is enmity against God. We can't make it better. This is not a process. It is a moment of faith that says, "I believe Jesus, I believe the Word of God. He can and will do it."

That's the challenge: will we believe in Jesus' blood or the devil's false doctor? The prescription of the false doctor says, "If you just read the Bible a little more. If you just pray a little harder. If you just go to church a little more. It will make your heart holy." No, friend, it won't. While these are all things we should do because we are "seeking first the Kingdom of God," they can do nothing to purify the heart.

The deceitful thing about the devil's doctor is this; it'll make you feel better about yourself. It will hopefully help you grow some spiritually. But it is only a substitute when it comes to purifying the heart. It bypasses the blood of Jesus, the only cure for the sinful heart. It's a trick of the devil to get you off track, get your eyes off Jesus, and eventually discourage you as the carnal nature continues to manifest itself in your life.

The thing about this second work of grace, this heart cleansing, and being filled with the Holy Spirit, is this is something only God can do. Just as you could not do anything to save yourself from your sins, neither can you do anything good enough to clean up your heart. Only the Great Physician can replace that dirty, carnal, sinful heart and make it clean, new, and pure. Only Jesus! Run to Him in faith!

It seems so simple compared to works and yet so many miss it. As Paul says to the Galatians, I say to the Church world, "Are ye so foolish? having begun in the Spirit, are ye now made perfect [complete] by the flesh?" (verse 3)

If Doctor Works doesn't work, the devil has many other "doctors" to give us other prescriptions for the cleansing of the heart. He sends us in many other directions, always away from Jesus.

Dr. Confusion

The devil just wants us to come up short and to place our faith somewhere else; to turn us away from the blood and from the simplicity of faith in that blood. The devil doesn't really mind if we believe in the infallibility of Scripture, or the deity of Christ, or the virgin birth, or even the new birth. But when it comes to entire sanctification, the removal of his ally from our heart, he'll fight you tooth and nail.

He comes to preachers, to those called to preach the whole counsel of God, and tells us, "Man, if you preach or teach that, you'll lose everyone. You will never be able to grow your church. You won't have any friends. Your wife will leave you, and the Church world will fight you." (And he's right about that!) He intimidates us with fearful thoughts to try to keep us from sharing this truth of holiness which is found in Jesus. Sadly, many preachers have, and are, caving to those thoughts.

He does the same thing to hungry Christians. Even if you sit in church week after week, he'll do his best to confuse the whole thing when it's as simple as faith in the blood of Jesus to do it. I Thessalonians 5:24 says, "Faithful is he that calleth you, who also will do it." What does the devil do?

First, he confuses God's created humanity with the devil's implanted carnality.

This is the number one error that Doctor Confusion plants in people's minds. I've been in the ministry for nearly forty years and we fight this confusion all our lives.

The devil, the head "physician," Doctor Confusion himself, comes and tries to get us to associate our humanity with carnality so closely that people conclude that you cannot separate the two. He then tells us we can't be pure. Why? Because you're human. It's like Job's counselors, most miserable. Calvinism has bought into this lie, lock, stock, and barrel.

We need to understand this error from Scripture and logic. Part of this error is due to the King James use of the word *flesh,* which sometimes refers to our bodies and other times refers to the sinful nature. Other versions generally have clarified that. Logically, though, it just doesn't make sense. When Doctor Confusion comes and says that, we need to logically answer, "Wait a minute. Who created humanity? God did. Was humanity pure for a time before Adam and Eve sinned?" The answer must be Yes, if we believe our Bibles at all.

Then, "Do you believe that Jesus Christ was God come in the flesh? That He partook of humanity?" Because if He did then humanity cannot be sinful, because the Bible tells us that "in Him is no sin" (I John 3:5). He was human and the Bible is very clear about that as well. He wept, hurt, loved, had emotions, bled, and died. He was completely human. Adam, Eve, and Jesus show us that holiness and humanity are completely compatible!

Let us take the thought a little further. If our humanity is sinful then God, the Creator of humanity, was the Creator of sin, because He created humanity. Humanity is redeemable; carnality is not. Paul was correct in Romans 6:6, "...that the body of sin [carnality] might be destroyed..."

God's whole program of salvation is to take our humanity and to cleanse from us the infection and nature of carnality and restore our humanity to purity. The only thing that makes us unacceptable to God is sin and only the blood of Jesus is sufficient to deal with sin.

It is not our finiteness, our mistakes, our lack of perfect understanding, performance, or memory. That's humanity. It is carnality, our sinfulness, that big No to God in the heart, that fights Him. God wants to deal with that. Carnality is the very image of the devil in our heart. It's not the devil, but *it's the very likeness of him and it has got to go.* Only faith in the blood of Jesus can cleanse that. We will never have the victory God wants us to have in life until God has victory in our hearts.

My question is always, Why would any Christian, desiring to be all that God wants him to be, want to live short of the total victory found in Jesus? Many settle to live in Romans chapter 7, instead of moving on to the victorious life in Romans chapter 8. Even in Romans 6 Paul writes this: "Being then made free from sin, ye became the servants of righteousness."

Dr. Confusion! Don't let him work on you. Carnality is not humanity. As I heard Dr. Jimmy Lentz once say, "God will never take anything out of you in sanctification that He put into you at creation." Even our desires are normal. They are temptable, but they are not sinful.

The devil knows that if we are not cleansed and given new and pure hearts, there is a good chance we'll fall back. It may be just in heart, as Stephen said about the Israelites in Acts chapter 7: "in their hearts [they] turned back again into Egypt." The devil is not opposed to that one bit; in fact, he wants that to happen.

He likes "sinning Christians." He likes those who believe that all there is in life is to continue in sin and to live with the constant inward warfare. Not me! I don't want failure. I don't want that constant inward battle. *I want victory.* I want to love God with all my heart and live like it. I want a Deliverer, a Savior, a Redeemer, that is *greater than the devil.*

I don't want to preach a Jesus that can't undo in me all that the devil did in me. I want to preach Someone Who is greater and more powerful than any foe we might face in this life.

We'll continue to look at some of these "doctors" in the next chapter, but for now, have you placed your faith in Jesus or Dr. Works? *I'll just do more of this and a little less of that.* That's not a bad thing, but it cannot cleanse the heart from sin. Oh, friend, stop working on it and trust Jesus to cleanse your heart. Don't come short of the simple answer, faith in Jesus!

Dr. Confusion. It's just human to continue to sin. No, friend, it's sinful, it's carnal, to continue in sin. It is human to walk with God, to know Him, and to love Him. That's where we need to be living and where I want to live. This is not about being human but being sinful. It is not our infirmities nor desires, it's sin God want to deal with. Don't let Dr. Confusion work on you. Let Jesus. He will, if you place your faith in Him to do it.

8
A Fresh Vision of the Enemies of Holiness (Part 2)

8
A Fresh Vision of the Enemies of Holiness (Part 2)

"O foolish Galatians, who hath bewitched you, that ye should not obey the truth, before whose eyes Jesus Christ hath been evidently set forth, crucified among you? This only would I learn of you, Received ye the Spirit by the works of the law, or by the hearing of faith? Are ye so foolish? having begun in the Spirit, are ye now made perfect by the flesh?" (Galatians 3:1-3)

IN THE LAST CHAPTER I mentioned two false "doctors," Dr. Works and Dr. Confusion. Dr. Confusion isn't done yet. Yes, he will confuse humanity and carnality— the fact that one is good, God-created, humanity; the other bad, devil-caused, carnality. Humanity is redeemable and carnality is not. Humanity can receive a new, pure heart; carnality must be put to death. Another remedy Dr. Confusion likes us to get us off track with is...

Confusing maturity with purity.

There is a great difference in growing in the grace and knowledge of Jesus, and the purity of the heart. The purifying of the heart is done instantaneously by faith in the blood of Jesus. In a moment of time you are cleansed from all sin and filled with the Holy Spirit. Maturity is a lifetime of growth in Jesus that began the day you were born again and will continue all the days of your life.

Purity is the work of God in the heart that can only be done through faith in the cleansing blood of Jesus. Maturity is a work in one's life that comes from reading your Bible, prayer, and the continued help of the Holy Spirit. Purity comes through entire sanctification; maturity comes through the ongoing process of sanctification.

The old illustration is true, "You can't grow carnality out of the heart any more than you can grow weeds out of a garden." Carnality, like weeds, must be removed, pulled up and taken out of the heart and done away with. Now, I've pulled weeds from gardens. If you don't root up those weeds completely and just pull one here or there, they'll take over your garden.

I heard one of my superintendents, Rev. Max Morgan say, "Carnality is like an octopus, it has too many arms. And while you may work on and pray about one manifestation, another pops up." You may pray about pride, think you're licking it, and then up comes selfishness. You pray about your selfishness, and think you have that licked, and up comes love of money. You pray about your love of money and up comes bitterness, lust, or carnal anger. It never ends. There are just too many arms.

I also heard him say, "It's like a one-fingered man trying to play a piccolo; you don't have enough fingers to cover all the holes." You cannot find victory in this battle with carnality by cutting off one arm at a time. You must slay the octopus between the eyes, at the source, the head.

You must kill the whole root of carnality or you'll spend your whole life fighting its arms or trying to cover holes.

This enmity must be dealt with at its source. The source is the sinful nature and only the blood of Jesus can kill it. This sinful nature must be uprooted, cleansed, by faith in the blood of Jesus. Really, the analogy of the weed and the garden goes even further. Because it is enmity against God, just like weeds in a garden, it will hinder your growth by taking away from the full nutrition that God wants to give you though His Word, and through His Spirit. It will suck the spiritual life out of you.

And you'll find yourself in and out of prayer, in and out of reading your devotions, in and out of the joy and strength of the Lord to live a victorious life. Instead of having good consistent victory you will find yourself always going back to battle the attitudes of the heart. A good picture of this warfare is given to us by Paul in Galatians 5:17; he writes: "For the flesh desires what is contrary to the Spirit, and the Spirit what is contrary to the flesh. They are in conflict with each other [at enmity with one another], so that you are not to do whatever you want."

I don't want to live there, do you? Paul goes on in Galatians 5:24 to give us the answer: "Those who belong to Christ Jesus have crucified the flesh with its passions and desires."

Which brings the logical question, can anything crucified still be living? Even Jesus Himself truly died on the cross. You just don't come back from a crucifixion, still living. Neither does the sinful nature. Amen!

Don't let Dr. Confusion fool you on the matter. Humanity and carnality are not the same. Maturity and purity are two completely different aspects of God's work. Purity in our hearts, maturity in our lives. Purity is instantaneously done by the blood of Jesus, for His "blood cleanseth us from all sin" (I John 1:7).

Maturity is a lifelong growth process done with the help of the Holy Spirit.

I heard my father, Harold Moyer, say in a message one time, "Aimless consecrations end up with endless reconsecrations." We need that understanding again in these days. Romans 12:1 says we need to "present [our] bodies as a living sacrifice, holy, acceptable unto God, which is [our] reasonable service." This presentation is to be a once-for-all decisive act, never to be taken back. Reconsecration is never taught in Scripture.

We, too often, are like John "Uncle" Kunkle once said, "Too many people are like the kamikaze pilot who flew a hundred missions, they never die." May God help us again these days to see the purity of heart that comes from a death to sin, self, and this world.

The devil is not through yet with his bag of tricks. If Dr. Works and Dr. Confusion don't do the job, he sends another "doctor" with two names:

Dr. Purgatory/Dr. Death.

I'm doing my best by Scripture and reason to clarify things that people seem to lean on and be confused about when it comes to be entirely sanctified and filled with the Spirit, cleansed from all sin, and that this work of dealing with sin is solely based by faith in the work of the Lord Jesus Christ on the cross of Calvary.

The devil wants us to believe and concede that we must live with the battle against inward sin all our lives and that Jesus' blood cannot cleanse us of sin in this life; that we cannot have clean and pure hearts in this life; that we cannot live in good victory in this life.

He then comes and tells us that this is a lifelong battle that you cannot be free of until you physically die. Then you'll be set free. We need to understand this thought process as well. To be released from the body, which Christ Himself experienced, is one thing, but to be released and delivered from carnality is a completely different thing.

For instance, the answer for the sinful nature in the Catholic faith is a place they call *purgatory.* Described in their own words it is a "place or means of purification." It's a place where a cleansing process is to happen. I am not an expert here, but from my understanding, this doctrine teaches that Christians are not ready for heaven when they die, so they are sent to an intermediate place where sin can be completely taken care of by suffering. I thought Jesus suffered and died in my place? No, we are told we must go to purgatory, that sin still must be cleansed, because Jesus didn't get the job done through the cross.

The amount of time we spend in purgatory is determined by how much good you did while you were alive. After you die the time is shortened by how many prayers, masses, and good deeds are done by your family and friends on your behalf. Two things: First, Purgatory is not supported by the Scriptures. Secondly, to depend on others and what they can do for me is sad, undependable, and dependent on the work of men rather than the shed blood of Jesus. Besides, what happens if others don't give? *I might stay in there a long, long time.* The answer is not Purgatory.

There is a more Protestant mainstream belief that we cannot be free from the sinful nature until death. Therefore, death removes the sinful nature. This is Calvinism's only answer. This belief is that we cannot be free from the sinful nature if we are alive and as long as we are in this human body.

Once again, let us follow some logical conclusions concerning the belief that death is the only answer to the sin problem. When I've had conversation with those with this belief, they usually will quote some Scriptures, and one of them is usually Romans 8:8 — "So then they that are in the flesh cannot please God."

They don't understand it's speaking of the flesh as the sinful nature. They also forget what it says in Hebrews 11:5, speaking of Enoch, "...he had this testimony, that he pleased God." Giving them the benefit of the doubt, it may sound like a good argument. The problem is they don't quote Romans 8:9, and seem to forget it is even there— "But ye are not in the flesh [what?], but in the Spirit, if so be that the Spirit of God dwell in you. Now if any man have not the Spirit of Christ, he is none of his."

I repeat again, there is nothing sinful about this body of ours. As we mentioned, Jesus had a body exactly like ours. Yes, He got weary, tired, sad, happy, frustrated, and angry, but there was no sinful nature in Him at all. Adam had no sin in him, either, until after the Fall. Holiness and humanity are completely compatible with the human body, with its natural desires. The body is not sinful. Our desires, in fact, are a gift of God. Yes, the devil likes to tempt us through our desires, but the desires themselves are part of God's gift to us in the creation of humanity.

What do we then do with Zechariah's prophecy concerning Jesus in Luke 1:74, 75— "That he would grant unto us, that we being delivered out of the hand of our enemies might serve him without fear, in holiness and righteousness before him, *all the days of our life*" (emphasis added).

It is only the corruption of sin that has tainted humanity and put a bent in us to commit sinful acts. It is not a departing from humanity that we need, but a removal of the sinfulness. We need to be purified in heart. Let's take the logic a little further.

If we believe that we are not set free from our sinfulness until death, there is some amazing logic that must take place, or should I say *illogic*. God's Word tells us in Romans 5:12 that "by one man sin entered into the world, and death by sin." Romans 6:23 adds, "the wages of sin is death." If the cause of death is sin as it is clearly stated, then can death destroy, or get out of us, what it caused?

Let us take it a step further. If death releases us from our sinful natures, then the one who caused death would be our sanctifier. Was it not Satan who brought death into this world? If so, then it would be Satan's work, not Christ's, that would free us from sin.

Let us take it another step further. If death frees us from sin, and as it says it I Thessalonians 4:3 that "...this is the will of God, even your sanctification," and death brings that, wouldn't the best thing that could ever happen to us would be to get saved and die? Then we could be free from the sinful nature and go to heaven. Obviously, I'm being a little facetious, but it is the logical outcome of that belief.

The Bible clearly teaches us that we can be free from all sin. It is not by Purgatory or death. It is by faith in the love, grace, and cleansing power of the blood of Jesus Christ. Like the song "There is Power in the Blood" says, "Would you be free from your burden of sin, your passion and pride? There's power in the blood." The Hebrew writer put it this way: "Wherefore Jesus also, that he might sanctify the people with his own blood, suffered without the gate" (Hebrews 13:12). His people are those who have repented, been born again, and who have experienced His incredible love.

Do we really think Jesus would have died and suffered for something that didn't matter that much? Do we really believe He would suffer and die for something that He couldn't provide or that we didn't need in this life? What He did was suffer and die for something — our cleansing — that is so vital to us in this life.

This is not just a "pet belief." This isn't just a special doctrine to make us different from other churches or denominations. This is the plain teaching of God's Word, and it's God's will for His people, to entirely sanctify them, to purify their hearts by faith.

The devil has many false cures. We've mentioned Dr. Works, Dr. Confusion, Drs. Purgatory and Death and discovered they are not the answer to our need. Let me mention one more.

Dr. Imputation

This belief generally comes in two thoughts. One of Satan's and Calvinism's most popular method of dealing with the sinful heart is this: "Well, God just doesn't see it. You are covered by Christ's righteousness, even though you yourself are not righteous." He can't see it. He's blinded to it. He's not looking at our hearts but at Christ's righteousness.

The Bible is very clear that God does not look at the outward appearance, but at the heart— our heart, not Christ's. David said in Psalm 51, "Create in me a clean heart, O God." Why pray that if it were not possible? What do we do with all the Biblical descriptions from God's Word concerning men's hearts: *pure, clean,* and *holy?* If something is just covered over can it be described by any of those terms?

The other popular method of dealing with the sinful heart is to say Christ's righteousness is imputed to us. That means it is put to our account and that's all that matters anymore. It's credited to us. Therefore, I can still live in sin, but it doesn't matter; it doesn't count, because I'm holy by proxy. But again, is that heart clean, pure, holy, or cleansed? No! You cannot impute something without there at the same time being an imparting. If you believe that, I would like you to take all your money and put it on my account at the bank, impute it to me, and let's see whose it is the next day.

The point of all this discussion is the same. There is no other method that can cleanse and purify the sinful heart, the sinful nature, than faith in the blood of Jesus. His blood deals with the heart while all the other "doctors" bypass it.

Purity of heart— cleansing, purging, entirely sanctifying the heart— can only come through faith in the work and blood of Jesus on Calvary. There is no other provision; there is no other cure. Everything else comes up short and fails to deliver us from the problem itself. In every case, all the other methods and beliefs are bad substitutes and bypass the power of God to do the work in us we need. In every case they take our eyes off Jesus and place our faith in imaginary "doctors" who are not able to meet our need at all. They sidetrack us from the real Answer.

I've only mentioned a few of the false doctors the devil likes to send our way; there are many more; Dr. Tongues, Dr. Emotionalism, and Dr. Legalism, among others. Let us not be discouraged. There is an Answer. There is a true Doctor. *There is Jesus.*

What Does Dr. Jesus Do?

Jesus said in Matthew 5:8 in the Sermon on the Mount, "Blessed *are* the pure in heart: for they shall see God" (emphasis added). If this was the only verse in the Bible, I'd still believe it, pursue it, and find it by experience, because He says, then we'll see Him. As one song says, "I want to see Jesus, the one who died for me."

David prayed in Psalm 51:7, "Purge me with hyssop, and I shall be clean: wash me, and I shall be whiter than snow." The word *purge* means, "to be free from moral defilement; to make free from something unwanted; to get rid of." *The heart is purged.* That's the work Jesus wants to do in us!

David continues, in Psalm 51:10, "Create in me a clean heart, O God." The word *clean* means "to be free from dirt or pollution, free from contamination or disease, free from error or blemish." *The heart is clean.* That's the work Jesus wants to do in us!

Peter said in Acts 15:8, 9, "And God, which knoweth the hearts, bare them witness, giving them the Holy Ghost, even as He did unto us; and put no difference between us and them, purifying their hearts by faith." The word *purify* means "to make clear, to free or clear from defilement or imperfection." *The heart is purified.* That's the work Jesus wants to do in us!

Paul prays in I Thessalonians 5:23 that "the very God of peace sanctify you wholly." The word *sanctify* means "to make holy, purify, to set free from sin and to set apart as holy." *The heart is sanctified.* That's the work Jesus wants to do in us!

John clearly states in I John 1:7, "the blood of Jesus Christ his Son cleanseth us from all sin." The word *cleanseth* means "to purify, to rid of impurities, to remove, to cleanse." In this passage that means continuously. *The heart is cleansed and kept clean.* That's the work Jesus wants to do in us!

Jesus said it. David said it. Peter said it. Paul said it. And John said it. *God wants us to have clean, pure, sanctified hearts.* Paul goes on in I Thessalonians 5:24 to say, "Faithful is He that calleth [us], who also will do it." He is referring us back to I Thessalonians 4:7 where he wrote, "For God hath not called us unto uncleanness, but unto holiness." Then he adds these words in verse 8: "He therefore that despiseth, despiseth not man, but God, who hath also given unto us his Holy Spirit."

The Scriptures leave no question as to what God wants to do in us. He wants to give us, through faith in the blood of Jesus, clean hearts, pure hearts, cleansed hearts, purged hearts, and sanctified hearts.

I quote all these Scriptures because the devil will do everything he can to get us to do something else with the sinful heart, other than letting the blood of Jesus cleanse it by faith. This is a work Jesus lived for and died for. John the Baptist tells us in John 1:29 that Jesus came to take away the sin of the world.

The devil comes to get us to try everything else to take it away. He will tell us to polish it up and give it some culture, to control it, to make it less noticeable. But does that take it away? He will tell us to suppress it, work on it, just live with it, go to church more, pray more, and as one version puts it, "to render it inoperative". Never mind that the Greek word means "to abolish, cease, and destroy." But "to render it inoperative," does that take it away?

Obviously not! We need more than just to take away its power. That's impossible. It is enmity against God, not subject to the will of God, and neither indeed can be. We need it cleansed. There is only one remedy for the sinful nature: faith in the blood of Jesus. *That blood can purify, cleanse, purge, and sanctify the heart.* Amen!

Everything else comes short and fails to deliver us from the problem itself. All the false "doctors" are exactly that— false. They are bad substitutes that bypass the power of God to do the work we need to have done to have clean, new, and purified natures.

Here's how you recognize a substitute: It is any system of religion or doctrine that bypasses the personal crucifixion of sin in the Believer's heart by the cleansing blood of Jesus. All else is an enemy of true holiness. *No cross, no crown.*

A.W. Tozer said this: "You cannot have a glorious resurrection until you've had a crucifixion." You cannot have a holy heart, a pure heart, a heart cleansed from all sin until you believe in the blood of Jesus to complete this work in you.

It is not by works, growth, confusion between humanity and carnality, purity and maturity, death, the fires of Purgatory, nor imputation. This is the work of

God through Jesus by faith. You can never be free on a substitute. Dear Christian, have you placed your faith in Jesus for this work of cleansing to be done in you?

9
A Fresh Vision of the Last Enemy of Holiness

9

A Fresh Vision of the Last Enemy of Holiness

"Now the serpent was more subtil than any beast of the field which the LORD God had made. And he said unto the woman, Yea, hath God said, Ye shall not eat of every tree of the garden? And the woman said unto the serpent, We may eat of the fruit of the trees of the garden: But of the fruit of the tree which is in the midst of the garden, God hath said, Ye shall not eat of it, neither shall ye touch it, lest ye die. And the serpent said unto the woman, Ye shall not surely die: For God doth know that in the day ye eat thereof, then your eyes shall be opened, and ye shall be as gods, knowing good and evil. And when the woman saw that the tree was good for food, and that it was pleasant to the eyes, and a tree to be desired to make one wise, she took of the fruit thereof, and did eat, and gave also unto her husband with her; and he did eat. And the eyes of them both were opened, and they knew that they were naked; and they sewed fig leaves together, and made themselves aprons. And they heard the voice of the LORD God walking in the garden in the cool of the day: and Adam and his wife hid themselves from the presence of the LORD God amongst the trees of the garden." (Genesis 3:1-8)

IN THIS CHAPTER WE GO back to the Garden of Eden to look at what is the last enemy of holiness. I want us to look at the core of carnality, the very central issue that must be dealt with if we are to be entirely sanctified.

I've heard a lot of sermons about what the core of the sinful nature is. I heard that it is pride, or that it's selfishness or self-centeredness. But behind the pride and selfishness, that one thing, that one last battle that must be fought in order to be cleansed of all sin, purified in heart, and filled with the Holy Spirit and living in victory — there is one thing that has to be dealt with.

I say it that way because behind every sin, behind every indication of carnality, and behind every sinful attitude that comes from the heart, is a specific cause. I remember when I was living as a teenager in California, I attended a junior high school called Peter Lassen. I attended also Hiram Johnson High School. It was, according to studies, one of the ten worst high schools in Northern California.

In those schools there were many ethnic groups. In fact, in my high school there were more minorities, as a whole, than whites. My best friend during those days was Mexican American. Because of all these ethnic groups there was a lot of tension and a lot of prejudice. On several occasions things got out of hand.

Fights, and literally riots, would break out— Black versus White, Mexican versus Chinese, Black versus Mexican. Sometimes it would get so bad that if you were Black, White, Mexican, or Chinese you wouldn't even go to the bathroom without support because you might get beat up.

On one occasion I remember things at school literally went crazy. *People went crazy.* Fights broke out. You didn't walk alone. If you didn't want to fight you pretty much had to stay home. During this particular time, they even cancelled school for a few days to calm things down.

When things finally got back under control, they found out it was just a few people, a few Blacks and Whites, that were causing all the trouble. They were the instigators and they were the ringleaders. They were the central cause of all the problems. Until they were found out, discovered, uncovered, and dealt with, nothing could be done to stop the carnage they had begun.

I say all that to say this: it is the same way with the sinful nature, carnality. Until we identify the cause, the core issue, we have no way of stopping all those manifestations of pride, selfishness, bitterness, love for money, love for the world, or any other ugly thing that comes out of the carnal heart.

It's that way with any disease, isn't it? You must find the source, the core problem, or else you'll simply be dealing with the manifestations of the disease. Our most damaging disease, if I can call it that, is the sinful nature. The carnal heart, the sinful heart; we must know the core cause of it so it can be dealt with.

We worry about a lot of things in Christianity. We deal with music tastes, worship styles, and what to wear and what not to wear. We busy ourselves with a lot of things that don't really matter. The only thing God wants to deal with is sin. Why? Because *sin separates us from Him, from Heaven, and from His love.*

I want to make a statement and then show you why it is Biblically correct. The very core of carnality and essence of carnality is unbelief. As I said, some may argue it is pride, selfishness, or self-centeredness, and can build a good case for those beliefs. But behind those desires is something else: unbelief. I use a familiar outline: is it Scriptural, Reasonable, and Experiential? I don't want you to just take my word for it.

Is it Scriptural?

I've thought about this for years, and especially as I entered the ministry. I've concluded that the core of the sinful nature is just plain old unbelief. We see it in its very essence in the temptation of Satan to Eve when he said, "Surely, hath God said...?" Those were Satan's very first words to her. These words were behind the whole temptation that was about to come.

What was Satan doing? He was creating doubt in God's Word and Who God is. It was the very essence of his own fall from heaven, when he thought that God wasn't God, and that he could become like Him. Satan hasn't changed his tactics one bit over the years. He is still trying to get us to deny the authority of God's Word. He is still trying to get us to doubt what God says is absolutely true and what Jesus came to do, can do, and will do.

It's even being debated today whether there are any absolutes or not. Where did that come from? *Not from God but the devil.* This battle is deeper than pride and selfishness. This is an attack on the Godhood of God, His character, and His Word.

We read clearly that God told Adam and Eve that "the day that thou eatest thereof thou shalt surely die" (Genesis 2:17). So cleverly and subtly has Satan done his work of sowing the poison of unbelief in people's hearts, that instead of millions of people weeping their way to the Almighty God for forgiveness and cleansing, thankful that Jesus has come and provided a full and free salvation, we find people rejecting Christ and feeling no need of the blood at all.

When heaven and hell are at stake, it defies all logic. People deny the creation. People deny the Incarnation.

People deny the birth of Christ, the life of Christ, the cross of Christ, the death of Christ, and the resurrection of Christ. Even in the Church they deny some of these things and the existence of hell.

They deny the punishment of sin. They deny that the wages of sin is death. They live in sin without worry, and without fear. Why? Because people just don't believe God. It's why it's so hard to win souls and bring them to true repentance.

I hope you are seeing it was unbelief in God's Word that caused Adam and Eve to eat the fruit. They just didn't believe God's Word. Eve believed Satan, the liar and father of lies. She believed the devil who said, *Surely you can disobey. You can sin against God, and not die.* Many Scriptures bear witness to this truth. While we will not deal with them all, let us look at Hebrews 3:19.

"So we see that they could not enter in because of unbelief."

The people of Israel could not enter Canaan. Why? *Because of unbelief.* The passage also states in verse 12, "Take heed, brethren, lest there be in any of you an evil heart of unbelief, in departing from the living God." Verse 18: "And to whom sware he that they should not enter into his rest, but to them that believed not?"

It was their experience all through the wilderness. The opening of the Red Sea, the manna from heaven, and the water from the rock— God was meeting their every need! He was fighting every battle they faced. Yet, when it was time to trust God to enter in, what happened?

We see the story. The twelve spies are sent out. God said, "Go in, possess the land. I will be with you. I'll go before you. Go on, take possession. *It's yours.*" They come back and ten spies say, "We can't enter in." Joshua and Caleb say, "Let's do it!"

What a picture this is. Belief said, "We are well able."

Unbelief said, "The cities are walled and very great." Belief said, "God is with us." Unbelief said, "We are but grasshoppers." Belief said, "The Lord will bring us in." Unbelief said, "We are not able to go in for they are of great stature, giants." (See Numbers 13.)

The first thing Jesus said in John 16:8,9, speaking of the ministry of the Holy Spirit— "he will reprove the world... of sin, because they believe not on me." Why? "...because they believe not on Me." Unbelief is God's description of sin which is the biggest battle there is. I hope you are seeing this. The core of carnality, of the sinful heart, is unbelief. It is enmity against God because it does not, and will not, believe Him.

No wonder then it is not subject to the will of God and neither indeed can be. (See Romans 8:7.) It doesn't believe Him. It is Scriptural.

It is reasonable.

"Come now, and let us reason together, saith the LORD..." (Isaiah 1:18) Let us just think this through. The Bible says in Hebrews 11:6, "But without faith it is impossible to please him: for he that cometh to God must believe that he is, and that he is a rewarder of them that diligently seek him [God]." The Bible clearly states that we are saved by faith. The Bible clearly states that we are sanctified by faith. The Bible clearly states that we are to pray in faith. The Bible clearly tells us that we are to live by faith.

If you were the devil, what's the only reasonable thing to sow in the hearts of people? Unbelief! He figured if he could do that, it would cut us off from being saved, sanctified, seeing answers to prayer, keeping grace on our souls altogether, and living in victory. All hope would be gone, and *we'd be his forever*. Why? Because as I John 5:4, 5 states, "...and this is the victory that overcometh the world, even our faith. Who is he that overcometh the world, but he that believeth that Jesus is the Son of God?" The devil's conclusion would be that without faith we could never please God.

If it were not for the fact of God's love, Christ's gift, and the Holy Spirit's ministry of grace, we would all be lost. The devil thought he had won the battle when he sowed unbelief into the heart of men. *But God.* The devil didn't figure on the Incarnation— God on earth! The devil didn't figure on the power of Christ's blood to forgive and cleanse. The devil didn't understand the fullness of God's love for His creation, and that He would provide enough grace to deliver us. The devil is smart, but he is not God. (This is another whole sermon in itself.)

But the idea of sowing unbelief into our hearts is just reasonable, from the devil's point of view, since everything about the Kingdom of God is wrought in faith. Unbelief is the opposite of faith.

A third thought:

It is experiential.

As Christians, what does our experience teach us? How did we get saved? By faith. At a point in time we confessed our sins and faith leapt up in our hearts and we believed God to forgive our sins and give us a new life, through the blood of Jesus. We never forget that time because the Holy Spirit bore witness to us that the work had been done. Amen!

How were we entirely sanctified and given new and clean hearts? The very same way— by faith. At a point in time we laid our whole sinful nature, our whole self, our whole world, at Jesus' feet. We laid our all on the altar and kept nothing back, and again, faith leapt up in our heart and we believed God for that cleansing and the fullness of the Holy Spirit. You never forget that time because the Holy Spirit bore witness to us that the work had been done. Again, I say, Amen!

It is true: whether getting saved or being entirely sanctified, unbelief is always the last battle to fight. We can die to self, to pride, to lust, to money, to things, to people, and to this world, but in the end, we still have to believe God can do the work of cleansing and filling that we are so desperately wanting.

I can't speak for everyone and we may say it in different ways, but I know in my own heart of hearts, and my own experience, that there was a moment where my faith had to overcome any unbelief so the work of God could be done. This work is Scriptural, reasonable, and experiential.

This is why so many fight and oppose the truth of holiness of heart and life, even when it is taught so in many ways in God's Word through stories, experiences, words, and illustrations. It is because unbelief in God's Word is the devil's last stronghold.

I share this one last thought:

What is unbelief?

Unbelief is a spontaneous (because we are born with it) *suspicion and distrust of God to fulfill His Word* in your life and in your heart. The sinful nature is enmity with God. It is a malicious slandering of the very character and will of God in your life.

This isn't some little doubt. This is an all-out attack on Who God is and calls Him a liar. Unbelief says, *God can't do that, He can't give you a clean heart.* The carnal nature, this unbelief, tries to rob God of His rights and will over your life and says, *You can't trust Him. You can't believe His Word. You cannot cast your all upon Him.*

Not only does it distrust God's Word, but unbelief also *suspects God's motives.* It is enmity. Every time the Lord comes and talks to your heart, says, "You've got a sinful problem going on in there. I want you to be mine completely, to commit your all— your family, your money, and your very self." The old man of unbelief will step up to the plate and say, "You can't trust God. He can't handle this. He can't handle your life. You know what's best for you. Don't trust God." Unbelief!

Unbelief also *suspects God's promises*. It attacks them. As a born-again Believer you will have a hard time believing God to be with you, to guide you, to strengthen you, to protect you and meet all your needs just because He's God, even though we have all the promises of His Word.

Despite His promises, the sinful heart of unbelief will make you reluctant to leave all and trust Him. To go to the mission field, to give up money and worldly security, to give up a home you worked so hard to get and let go and just follow Him. Unbelief will say, "Don't trust Him. I don't know about those promises. I don't think we can make it and go in that direction." The sinful heart is suspicious of God's promises.

Unbelief will tell you can't afford that share in a missionary because you'll starve to death. Yet you'll find yourself buying a new car, expanding your business, saving money for retirement and accumulating worldly goods, but that share will ruin you. You'll have to miss church on Sunday to work because you'll lose your job if you don't. You'll have to keep your tithe back because if you don't you won't get your bills paid. Unbelief will fight you every inch of the way and not trust God's promise that if we "seek ye first the kingdom of God… all these things shall be added unto you."

Unbelief will also lie to you about God's warnings, as well. Oh, how the sinful heart is deceitful above all things. The Bible tells us if we don't repent and turn from our wicked ways we'll die and go to hell forever. *Well, I don't know about that. A little sin here and there isn't any big deal. Would a loving God send you to hell over that?* The Bible tells us that the "wages of sin is death" (Romans 6:23). *Oh, no, it's not.* Yes, it is.

The Bible says that he that continues to commit sin is of the devil (I John 3:8). "Not me. I go to Church. After all, once saved, always saved." The Bible tells us that this unbelief is enmity against God, that the carnal mind will fight Him, and that this thing can overthrow our souls and bring us down. Unbelief will say, "Well, it'll be okay. You're good enough. You've got enough grace to make it. After all, you're better than So and So." Unbelief throws lies over God's Word, that says, "Follow peace with all men, and holiness [sanctification], without which no man shall see the Lord." "O, but I will."

Another thing unbelief does is continually test God. "Give me a sign. Show me some miracle, then I'll believe You." Oh, friend, do we not see the very core of unbelief, when after three years of healing, raising the dead, making people whole, sharing the Good News, they hung Jesus on the cross? And what did people say? "If you come off of there, then we'll believe you." No, they wouldn't. They would be looking for another sign or proof of Who He is.

Friend, I hope you are catching the horror of all this. Having this sinful heart of unbelief will fight God, exalt you above God, and cause you often to reason away God's clear Word, its demands and promises. It'll most likely take your soul if God doesn't cleanse and purify your heart.

This core of carnality, this unbelief, invaded our hearts in this life. The devil planted that in us in this life. It is in this life it needs to be dealt with so that we might be saved from our sins, cleansed of this unbelief in our hearts, and live in victory. *In this life.*

Oh, friend, God has a plan. Praise His name, *God has a plan.* It's called grace. Grace, not causing Him to overlook our sin or sinfulness, but to deliver us. There is prevenient grace, justifying grace, sanctifying grace, and keeping grace. May God help us to see that, through faith in Jesus' blood everything that was needed for deliverance from the penalty of sin, the power of sin, the practice of sin, and the very presence sin in our hearts, has been provided.

It is right here on this earth that we can be forgiven, cleansed, sanctified, filled with His Spirit, and live a life of victory. *It's all provided now.* Do you believe that?

Everywhere I've preached holiness, there are always those who say, "Well, I don't believe that. This isn't for me. I'll believe what I want to." It's not very long until they become like Peter— "Lord, I'll never fail You. I won't deny You. Others will but I won't. I'm man enough, and I've got enough grace." He didn't believe Jesus' words when he said that he would deny Him. In his unsanctified state he denied Christ three times. This is the constant fate of those who do not allow the blood of Jesus to purify their hearts.

Please, don't let unbelief tell you there is no need to be made holy in heart, that you don't need this second work of grace. Don't let unbelief tell you that you received all you need when you got saved and that you'll be okay. No! Believe God's Word! There is a cure for carnality by our faith in the purifying blood of Jesus that cleanses from all sin. Do you believe that?

Yes, you'll have to die to pride, evil anger, carnal lust, and the world, and whatever else God shows you is in your heart. Then in the end you come to this, the last battle, the last enemy, and the last issue: unbelief. If you need to, tell Him, "God, there is something in my heart that doubts you over this cleansing work. It's keeping me from believing and trusting and doing all you will in my life. O God, give me confidence in Your Word, in Your Son. Lord, 'I believe; help thou mine unbelief'" (Mark

9:24). Claim the promise, "Faithful is He that calleth you, Who also will do it" (I Thessalonians 5:24).

When it is all said and done, believing God, trusting God, is really the whole cure. Faith!

10
A Fresh Vision of How to be Entirely Sanctified

10
A Fresh Vision of How to be Entirely Sanctified

"And the very God of peace sanctify you wholly; and I pray God your whole spirit and soul and body be preserved blameless unto the coming of our Lord Jesus Christ. Faithful is he that calleth you, who also will do it." (I Thessalonians 5:23, 24)

THIS HAS ALWAYS BEEN one of my favorite passages. Paul is telling us that God is able and will do what He said was His will and His call to us earlier in this letter. Paul tells us in I Thessalonians 4:3, "For this is the will of God, even your sanctification, that ye should abstain from fornication." A few verses later in verse 7 he says, "For God hath not called us unto uncleanness, but unto holiness." These verses helped me much in believing God for the work He wanted to do in me.

One of the things that helped me most was that the word *sanctify* in I Thessalonians 5:23 is in what is called the "aorist tense." This means that the God of peace wants to, at a specific time, purify and cleanse my "whole spirit and soul and body." I don't believe, as some commentators have said, "Just because it's prayed for doesn't mean it can be done in this life." That would be the belief that David's prayer in Psalm 51 could not be answered. It would also be the belief that Paul was praying an impossible prayer for the Church, and that when Jesus prayed for this sanctification for His disciples, and us, in John 17, that could not be experienced, either.

This aorist tense means that I can be sanctified now, instantaneously, at a specific point of time. This experience of entire sanctification is not something I have to wait for. This blessing of the cleansing of my heart is not something I had to grow into but never know when it's completed. It's not an experience I have to wait for until I die. Amen! No, the God of peace can cleanse my whole spirit and soul and body right now, today, if I meet the conditions.

A second reason this verse helped and blessed me so much, is not only does it let me know this cleansing can be done in this life instantaneously, but that it continues and that I can be preserved blameless until the coming of the Lord. God can keep me clean. I can continue in this blessing by the strength and help of the Holy Spirit.

This is the experience John was talking about in I John 1:7, where he states that "if we walk in the light, as he is in the light, we have fellowship one with another, and the blood of Jesus Christ his Son cleanseth [present tense, continual action] us from all sin.

This is the experience Paul testified to in II Timothy 1:12 when he said, " for I know whom I have believed, and am persuaded that he is able to keep that which I have committed unto him against that day." I can keep the victory and I can walk in the light. Preservation is just like canning fruit; you cut the rotten stuff out first, then you preserve it. God preserves what He cleans up. Amen!

A third reason this verse blessed me and helped me, is that it is for every Believer. Paul didn't pray that the preacher be clean, but you can't be. He didn't pray for just this person or that one, but for the whole Church. This will of God, and this call of God, is the promise and prayer for all born-again Believers, men, women, and children. If you know Christ as your Savior, this prayer is for you. Amen!

A fourth reason this verse blesses me is because of the word *blameless*. It is not the same as *faultless*. I am encouraged that I don't stand before men but before God, who can see my heart motives for doing or not doing certain things. If I walk into a bar because God has led me to talk to people, which I have done, I don't have to feel guilty because of those who think I shouldn't ever enter places like that. When I preach what God lays upon my heart and people walk away, I don't have to worry what others think I should have preached and said in a different way.

I trust you understand what a blessing it means to walk blameless. I'm not going to be judged by my mistakes, lack of understanding, my human limitations, but by God Who is looking at my heart. I've come to learn over the years that we are a lot safer, concerning our salvation and eternal life with God's judgment, than we ever would be with man's.

A fifth reason I am blessed and helped is because of the 24th verse. Oh, friends, cling to it. "Faithful is He that calleth you, Who also will do it." God is faithful to do the work that He has willed for us and has called us to. I just praise God for that! God doesn't urge us, desire for us, prepare us, and send His Son to cleanse us from all sin by His own blood, and then say, "Oh, well, too bad, it can't be done. You'll just have to live with it. I was just kidding." No, He is faithful!

I remember when my daughter Julie was young. One

132 | A FRESH VISION

of the things we made sure our children did was clean up their plates. At one meal she hadn't cleaned up her plate and she looked at me with a smile and said, "Dad, I'm done!" After she saw on my face that she had fooled me, she said, "Just kidding!"

Friends, God doesn't kid with us. God doesn't play games with what His Only Begotten Son died to provide for us. His Son died and shed His blood to not only provide the forgiveness of sins, but to also provided a cure for sin in our hearts. I say, praise His name for that!

Let me emphasize once again, this blessing of entire sanctification, a cleansed heart from all sin, is for everyone who is born again. It comes by faith in the blood to do what the Bible has stated it can do. While we all will receive it by faith, we most likely will have differences in the way we feel, or the way we pray. But "Faithful is He Who calleth *you*, Who will also do it" (emphasis added).

What I'm saying is, don't try to pattern your experience by how someone else may testify to it. What they felt, what they dealt with, the words they prayed, may not be how God leads you to holiness of heart in your own life. I've seen it all, when people have been sanctified wholly and filled with the Spirit.

I've seen people cry in joy, jump for joy, shout for joy, and just sit there in peace and joy. No one necessarily acts any certain way when they experience entire sanctification. Reactions, whatever they might be, are only the result of the work, not a pattern to follow. They cannot be used to prove anything. This is an inward work.

Many souls miss the reality of this wonderful experience, this great blessing of God, because they are looking for something to happen instead of looking to Jesus for the blessing itself. There is no one outward sign that proves this work is done. This work isn't done in your head, or your hands, or your feet, or even your brain. It may affect all those things.

This is a work done in the heart. He wants to cleanse and sanctify your innermost being, what makes you what you are. Remember again the words of God to Samuel "Man looketh on the outward appearance, but the LORD looketh upon the heart" (I Samuel 16:7).

Entire sanctification is more than an emotional feeling. Entire sanctification is more than the clothes you wear. Entire sanctification is more than keeping certain standards and convictions. Entire sanctification is getting ahold of God's promises, and of the God of Peace Himself, to cleanse your heart from all sin.

The only thing we ought to know, or should want to know, or need to know, is the witness of the Holy Spirit that the work has been done. Like Elijah in the mouth of the cave, it is not in the wind, not in the earthquake, not in the fire, but in the still small voice of the Lord, "The work has been done." Yes, joy may follow that, shouts may follow that, tears of thankfulness may follow that, but it's those words we need to hear, "The work has been done."

In this last chapter I want to deal with the question, "How can I receive this blessing in my own soul, my own heart, and in my own life? What are the conditions God, through His Word, has laid out for me, that I might meet them and thus experience His faithfulness in cleansing my heart?" I trust I can keep this very simple.

The first step to being entirely sanctified is to know that we are saved, born again, and a child of God.

We must be born of the Spirit before we can be baptized of the Spirit. Never in Scripture are sinners ever called unto holiness of heart; always to repentance. Jesus was clear when He said in John 14:17, speaking to His disciples, "Even the Spirit of truth; whom the world cannot receive, because it seeth him not, neither knoweth him: but ye know him; for he dwelleth with you, and shall be in you."

Jesus was clear in John 17:9 as He prayed for this great blessing for His disciples. "I pray for them: I pray not for the world, but for them which thou hast given me; for they are thine."

The simple question we must answer is this: Am I saved? Am I born of the Spirit? Has there been a time in your life when you got alone with God and repented of your sins and asked God to forgive you, to live within your heart, and resulted in you becoming a new creation with old things passed away and all things new? Is that experience real, up-to-date, and ongoing today?

If you can answer Yes to those questions this blessing is for you! This is the first place we must start. The blessing of entire sanctification is a family blessing. We must be part of the family of God before we can receive the inheritance of holiness in our heart. We must pass from death into life before we can become the "living sacrifice" that Paul speaks of in Romans 12:1.

The second step in being entirely sanctified is you must walk in the light that you have received from the Holy Spirit and God's Word.

I've been in the ministry long enough to know that there are many people who spend their entire lives saying, "Well, God hasn't shown me that yet." We must be honest with the Word and ourselves. We have seen it clearly throughout many of the verses quoted in this book. Just this one, "This is the will of God, even your sanctification" (I Thessalonians 4:3), ought to be enough.

If we simply walk in the light as He is in the light, we will have fellowship with one another, and His blood will cleanse us from all sin. We don't have to understand all of it doctrinally. We must trust Him and His Word and claim the promise of I Thessalonians 5:24 that "He will do it."

Did not Jesus say in John 14:15, "If ye love me, keep my commandments"? Don't born-again people love the Lord and want to obey the Lord? Surely, they do! What about some of these commandments and statements?

"Be filled with the Spirit" (Ephesians 5:18). Or this one? "But tarry... until ye be endued with power from on high" (Luke 24:49). Or this one: "Who shall ascend to the hill of the Lord? Or who shall stand in His holy place? He that hath clean hands and a pure heart..." (Psalm 24:3, 4) Or this one: "Follow peace with all men, and holiness, without which no man shall see the Lord" (Hebrews 12:14). Or our text, "Faithful is He that calleth you, Who will also do it" (I Thessalonians 5:24).

If we are truly born again there must be a desire to walk in the light, to claim His promises, to obey His will and to be all that God would want us to be. Walk in the light, my friend. If need be, refer back to chapter 8, "What does Dr. Jesus do?"

You are saved, ready to walk in light, what's next?

To be entirely sanctified you must hunger and thirst for it.

During the Sermon on the Mount— just before we see the wonderful promise in Matthew 5:8, "Blessed are the pure in heart: for they shall see God" — is verse 6, where we read these words from Jesus: "Blessed are they which do hunger and thirst after righteousness: for they shall be filled." Now, that's a promise we ought to claim! "They shall be filled." Sounds so good, doesn't it?

As born-again Believers, do we not hunger to have a deeper walk with God? Do we not hunger for the blessing of righteousness, holiness, and purity of heart? Surely we do, for we want to see God. Jesus explained this hungering and seeking heart in Luke 11. In the story He talks about a son wanting some bread and asked if the father would give him a stone. Or if he was hungry for fish, would the father give him a serpent? Or if he was hungry for an egg, would the father give him a scorpion?

Jesus then says this: "If ye then, being evil, know how to give good gifts unto your children: how much more shall your heavenly Father give the Holy Spirit to them that ask him?" This hungering is deeper than most people realize. This is coming to the point of laying everything on the table, of sin, of self, and of this world, and saying, I want this blessing, this fullness, this cleansing, no matter the cost. It's the hunger and thirst of the soul. *It's a consecration of all to trust in Him.*

This is what Paul was referring to, so that he could testify in Galatians 2:20, "I am crucified with Christ: nevertheless I live; yet not I, but Christ liveth in me: and the life which I now live in the flesh I live by the faith of the Son of God, who loved me, and gave himself for me."

If you have a desire for the Holy Ghost, for righteousness, for cleansing, claim the words, "how much more shall your heavenly Father give the Holy Spirit to them that ask him?" Which brings us immediately to the next step.

To be entirely sanctified we must ask.

It almost seems foolish to even mention it. It is so simple and wonderful. In that same passage from Luke 11 Jesus gives us these promises: "Ask, and it shall be given you; seek, and ye shall find; knock, and it shall be opened unto you" (Luke 11:9). If our hungering and thirsting haven't led to asking, we have not yet truly hungered and thirsted for righteousness.

This experience of being filled with the Spirit and having the heart cleansed from all sin is not something you can just sit back and hope for. It's not something you hope to grow into. It's not something you can earn by good works. It's not something you can purchase. Only God can do this work and it comes through faith in the blood of His Son to do it. So you must ask Him, seek Him, and knock until it is opened.

Remember here again, verse 24, "Faithful is He that calleth you, Who will also do it." Add to that promise the words of Jeremiah 29:13, 14, where God said, "And ye shall seek me, and find me, when ye shall search for me [the God of peace] with all [hunger and thirst] your heart. And I will be found of you, saith the LORD..." Isn't that good!

Friends, how hard should it be for Christians, children of God, to ask for such a marvelous and wonderful gift? For cleansing? For the Holy Ghost fullness in our souls and lives, when both are available. "Ask, and it shall be given you; seek, and ye shall find; knock, and it shall be opened unto you" (Luke 11:9).

Be definite. This is a definite work; this is a cleansing work; this is a filling work; so ask for that. I've spent a lot of time at altars after preaching a message on holiness only to find people meandering all over the place with their prayers asking for help, asking for health, asking to get out of some problem, or to get through some spiritual trial. This is definite seeking for a definite and particular blessing of God, a clean heart filled with His Spirit.

This is a prayer for the cleansing blood of Jesus to be applied to your heart to cleanse it from all sin so that the Holy Ghost has every ounce of your being, thus filling you up with Himself. Ask, seek, and knock, for faithful is He Who calleth you.

The fifth step to be entirely sanctified is the step of faith.

This, as we mentioned in an earlier chapter, is always the last step. We must trust God completely. Therefore, we must die to unbelief, that says, "Hath God said?" This is of utmost importance, because we are sanctified by faith. This faith is more than just simply accepting it. This is a faith that goes beyond all emotions and feelings. This is a faith that goes beyond earthly things to grasp some heavenly unseen things. "Now faith is the substance of things hoped for, the evidence of things not seen" (Hebrews 11:1).

This is faith that comes to Almighty God, the God of Peace, and claims the promises of God based on the finished work of Christ at Calvary, for the purifying work of the Holy Spirit in your heart. This is faith in God that He is more than wanting and willing to do this work in you. It is an attitude of the heart and mind determined to experience this blessing.

It is an attitude that says, "I will not let thee go, except thou bless me" (Genesis 32:26). This faith says, "Even if I don't understand it all, *I must have it.*" This faith comes to the place where you want this blessing more than anything else in this world. This blessing is all that matters to you right now.

This is not seeking for power, although that will come. Power to be a witness. Power to have right attitudes in bad situations. Power to have a right motive in making decisions of life. That all comes, but that's not what you are seeking, for you are seeking the cleansing from all sin and the fullness of the Holy Spirit. This is not seeking to feel better, although that too will come!

This is seeking for God, just like David in Psalm 51, for a clean heart and a renewed right spirit within. Friend, if you want this blessing you must be born again, for this work of entire sanctification is offered only to Believers. You must walk in the light of God's Word. He wills this and calls us to this work.

You must hunger and thirst, and ask definitely, for this work, and let nothing else deter you from this specific work to be experienced.

Lastly, you must place your faith in God to do it. *He is faithful and He will!*

Made in the USA
Monee, IL
22 January 2024

52178287R00079